Cromosys Publication

Teach Yourself Adobe Flash

NIRANJAN JHA SHOWMAN

Cromosys Publication

Teach Yourself Adobe Flash

NIRANJAN JHA SHOWMAN

Founder - Niranjan Jha Showman

Education and Technology Research Center

Patankar Park, Nallasopara (W), Mumbai. +91-9561450045

Education, Technology, Publication, Healthcare, Newsmedia, Realtor, Filmmaking

www.facebook.com/cromosys

+91-9561450045
Learn Advanced Skills
And Get Job Instantly
GERMAN
Python
FRENCH
C++
SPANISH
Java
ENGLISH
HTML5
RUSSIAN
CSS
JavaScript
Cromosys
Education and Technology Research Center
Nallasopara (W), Mumbai

Learn Web Programming
Demo-Class Free
HTML
CSS
React
JavaScript
Typescript
Bootstrap
Cromosys
20 Years of Experience
Nallasopara (W), Mumbai
+91-9561450045

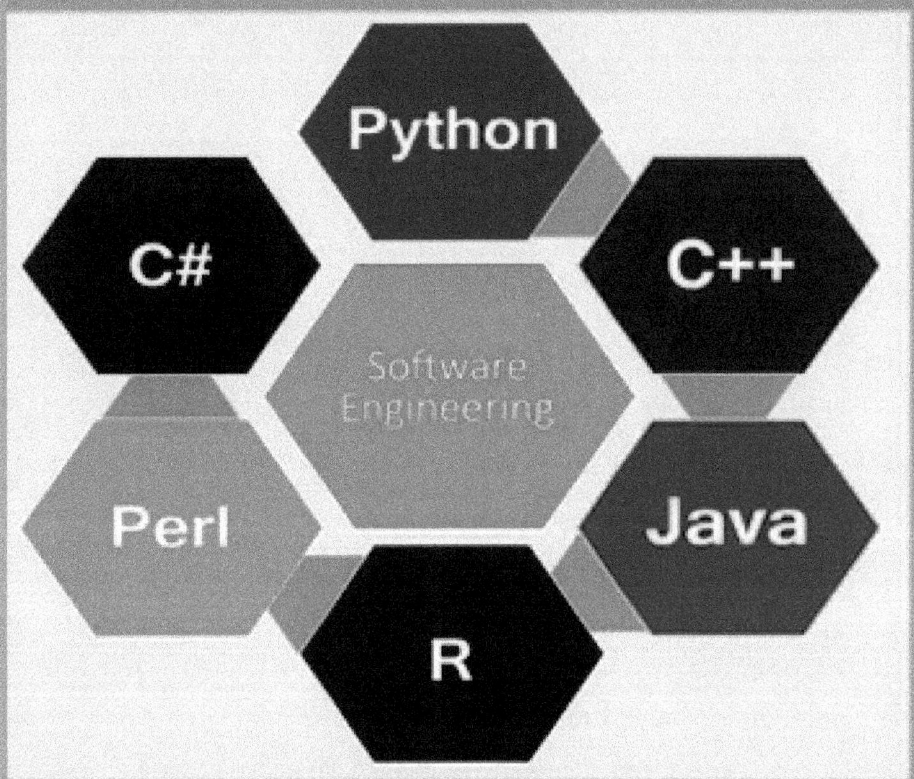

+91-9561450045
Learn Software Engineering
Demo-Class Free
Python
C#
C++
Software Engineering
Perl
Java
R
Cromosys
20 Years of Experience
Nallasopara (W), Mumbai
+91-9561450045

25 Years of Experience
Learn Visual Multimedia

● Animation VFX
● Movie Editing
● Game Development

Cromosys
+91-9561450045
Education and Technology Research Center
Nallasopara (W), Mumbai
www.facebook.com/cromosys

Jobs Available
For Candidates Who Know

German

French

Spanish

Vacancy in Germany, France, Spain
For Hospitality, Engineering, IT Sector
With Free Visa, Airfare and Accommodation

Cromosys
Education and Technology Research Centre
Nallasopara (W), Mumbai
+91-9561450045
20 Years of Experience

+91-9561450045
Foreign Languages Institute
German, French, Spanish
Basic and Advanced - All Levels
3 x 6 = 18 Courses
FRANCHISE
Business Offer
Teaching Materials Provided
We have 1 Million Students Globally
Great Income Assured
Global Exposure
Cromosys
20 Years of Experience
Nallasopara (W), Mumbai
+91-9561450045

Book: Teach Yourself Adobe Flash
Author: Niranjan Jha Showman
Publisher: Cromosys Publication
ISBN: Acquired
Date: 2020
Category: Computer Education

Preface

Cromosys Publication's **Teach Yourself Adobe Flash** book is an optimal quality guide to the beginners and advanced learners of Flash. We are the leading e-book publisher of languages and technology. Our research and education center working for last fifteen years has made tremendous effort to simplify the learning of Flash, and so we assure you that this book will walk you through in the friendliest manner in your entire course. Whether you are using Flash CS6 or the latest version, this book will make you a master of it in just one month. As today's world is the world of animation, everyone wants to create a moving, talking, and interacting visual expression. You may be interested in creating a movie, a game, or editing the content of a film or a website. That is where you need Flash to work for you, as it does all the work of this kind. The learning as well as working experience in Flash is amazing, astonishing, and exhilarating. As you start, you will feel that you've got a new horizon to present your imagination. It's cool, simple, and sublime!

Niranjan Showman, the author of this and fifteen others books available online, is the founder of Cromosys Corporation. His dedication in technological and linguistic research is significantly known to the millions of people around the world. This book is the creation of his avowed determination to make the learning of Flash easy to the people. After you install Flash software on your system, you just have to follow the instructions doing the same on your computer, and you will see that you are quickly learning everything. Just an hour of practice per day, and in a month of time you'll get a lot of knowledge, tips and tricks to work with this software. This is an unmatchable unique book of its kind that guarantees your success. The lessons are magnificently powerful to bring you into the arena of animation. Since it is the need of time, the people around the world have been sharpening their knowledge to be good in it. The still-image creation software like CorelDraw, Photoshop, and Illustrator are where you create pictures of your choice, but when you wish to make them move, talk, dance or do anything, there you need Flash. Don't think of Microsoft PowerPoint or Windows Movie Maker to do that job. What Flash does, no other software does. It is totally different. For instance, you want a car driven by from left to right side of the screen with its wheels moving. Do you think any other software can do that? No, absolutely not. Only Flash can do that and it can do it in just a minute of time. Like this, many other animations you can create following the steps given in the lesson of this book.

Now you may need to ask us whether it is necessary to have a good knowledge of CorelDraw, Photoshop, and Illustrator before starting Flash. For that, our answer is "no", not at all. Whether you know about any of this software or not, you can start learning Flash. It already has drawing tools in it. And to your surprise, Flash took birth in the house of Macromedia as still-image drawing software. The evolution brought it to be animation software. Moreover, you don't only create a movie in it, but publish its content to Web also, and that makes Flash more useful and stable. From the year of 2013, with the industrial growth, the learning of this tool is beneficial. Sometimes, only working knowledge doesn't work, and you feel that there is a lot more to explore. The accurate and profound knowledge of it has influenced zillions of minds today; therefore we conceived the idea of making this book a guideline for those who want to be perfect in Flash starting from real basic. One more thing is important to mention here that nobody can learn Flash while playing around it. People do learn other software like

PowerPoint and Windows Movie Maker with their very casual efforts, but Flash cannot be cowed down at all. It needs you to be curious, energetic, imaginative, and resolute. If you dare to be inattentive, you'll experience your own fall as you'll understand nothing of Flash. It is not like Microsoft Paint or word processor programs. It needs your attentive, continuous, controlled and patient efforts. Don't get carried away from the first lesson and start doing irrelevant things of your own as it happens because of vivaciousness of this software. You'll burst into laughter or start dancing seeing your drawing getting animated on Flash screen, but believe me, there would be still more to learn. For your technical information, Flash is one of the most important software of Multimedia and Animation learning.

Cromosys, our education and technology research center, saving human efforts from being wasted, is committed to help you gain profound and contemporary knowledge. The world growing with density has brought enormous opportunity to animation talents irrespective of their geographical boundaries. We strongly believe this book is useful for the people working for art and design, Web creation, media houses, entertainment world, and obviously for those who love animation. After you start the lesson, you don't need to worry about anything but just follow each and every step carefully. This e-book is designed to fulfill the instant need of learners in a very economical way, as it is easy to find on internet and affordable to buy and share. Cromosys, our path-breaking pioneer training institute for Computer Courses, English Speaking, Mass Communication, Foreign Languages, and Competition Coaching, is dedicated to enlightening human mind with educational endeavors, and we are doing the same for last successful fifteen years. We not only hope but believe that your success is in your hand now, as this book will take you miles ahead in your expectation. We always respect the views and comments of readers, so for any communication with regards to assistance, enquiry or collaboration, we are always there at your reach as it helps us improve our quality.

Niranjan Jha Showman
Founder: Cromosys Corporation
Web: facebook.com/cromosys
Contact no.   +91-9561450045
Email address: cromosys@yahoo.com

Books by the same author:
Teach Yourself Maya, Teach Yourself 3D Max, English Voice Accent and Pronunciation, Teach Yourself Spanish, Teach Yourself French, Teach Yourself German, English Word Power, Dynamic Grammar of English, English Dictionary of Modern Slang, Teach Yourself Tally, Teach Yourself Adobe Premiere Pro, Teach Yourself Adobe Flash, Teach Yourself Adobe After Effects, Teach Yourself Microsoft Word, Teach Yourself Microsoft Excel

Cromosys
Education and Technology Research Center
Education, Technology, Publication, Healthcare, Realtor, Filmmaking
Nallasopara (W), Mumbai, India

Caution: All the writing works that include all the educational, non-educational books, novels, and articles of the writer Niranjan Jha, are the published content of his registered magazine FACE OFF - Inventing Truth, which carries registration no. MAHENG12112/13/1/2009-TC and the endorsement no. 3244 28/5/2009 with the Ministry of Information and Broadcasting, Govt. of India. Any plagiarism in this regard will attract strict legal action. Any further publication of any of these books requires his written permission. Copyright certificate of this book is attached at the end of this book.

Lesson 1
Make an animation in a minute

Considering your curiosity to create an animation so that you can see how Flash works, here are the steps you can follow. As you read the steps, do it on your computer also because the steps written in technical manner is not only for reading.

1. Open Flash and select Flash File (ActionScript 3.0) from the Create New column of Flash's start page as shown in Picture 1.1 down below. See the pointer placed on ActionScript 3.0 option.

Picture 1.1

2. In case you don't find this option, click on File, New, and then select Flash File (ActionScript 3.0) from General tab. After you click ActionScript, your screen looks like as shown in picture 1.2

3. Press R key to turn your cursor into a rectangle tool. Now rectangle tool becomes active with your mouse pointer.

4. On the left side of the white board Stage, click and drag down to the right to draw a medium-sized rectangle. This will be how your animation begins.

5. Make sure that the Timeline panel is visible which a panel is with numbers written at the top. If is not visible, click Windows and Timeline.

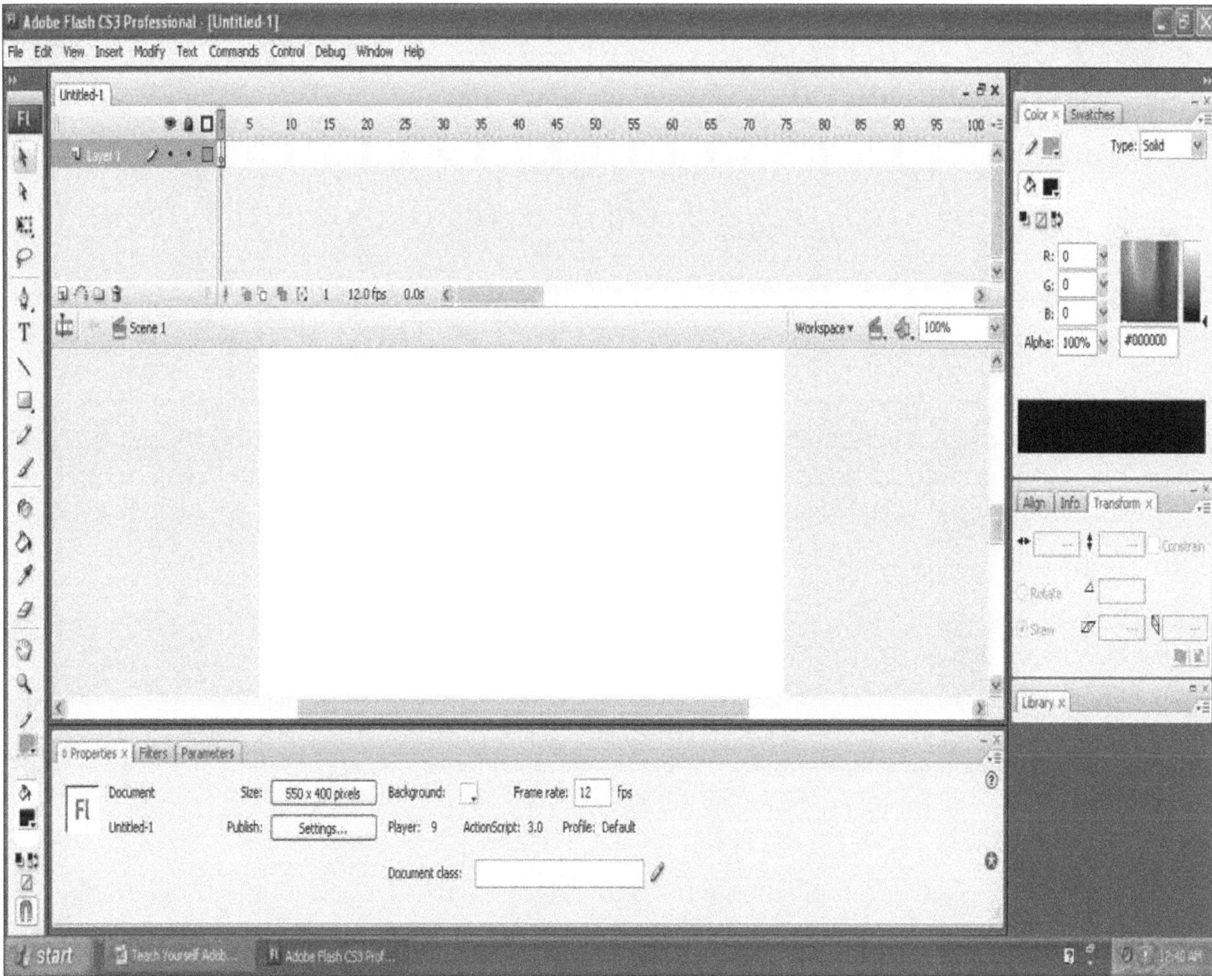

Picture 1.2

6. In the Frame of the Timeline, click the cell directly under 20, and press F7 which will insert a blank keyframe in it. This will be the end point of your animation to be drawn.

7. Now press O key to turn the cursor into an Oval tool. Go to the right side of the stage and drag to draw a medium-sized oval.

8. Now return to Frame 1 where the animation will begin, by clicking the dot underneath the Frame 1 in the timeline where your rectangle is.

9. Make sure the Properties panel is visible at the bottom as shown in picture 1.3. If it is not, select Windows, Properties, and Properties. The Properties panel changes based on what you select.

10. As you have already clicked on the dot underneath Frame 1 and its Properties panel is active at the bottom, go to Tween dropdown menu and select Shape. That's it!

11. Simply press Enter key to view your animation.

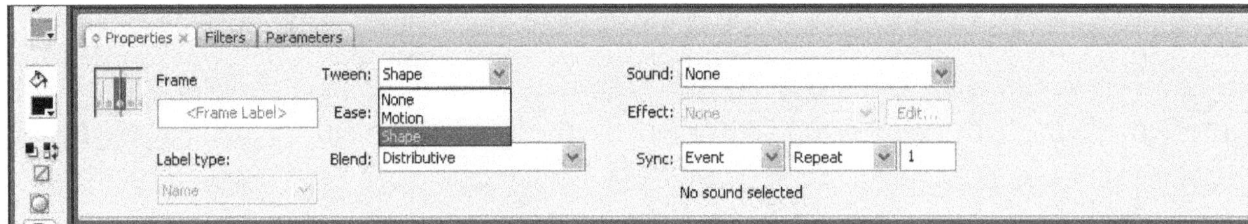

Picture 1.3

I am sure it would be quite fascinating to you. This is the beauty of Flash. Now, if you want to play it as a movie on the screen, just press Ctrl and Enter. If you go ahead and click on Save under File option, you'll save the file with .fla extension which can be opened in Flash anytime later for editing. If you click on Export and select Export Movie, the first option with .swf extension will save the file as a movie which you cannot edit but view it in Flash Player already installed in your system. If you select the second option and save it as .avi, you can see this movie in Media Player of Windows 7. Later, if you convert that file to .mpeg format using a third party converter on internet, you can see this movie on television.

Lesson 2
Simple Text animation

Now we are going to create a simple text animation of the word 'Cromosys'. You will see each letter coming on the screen at a certain interval. It is easy and simple to do so.

1. Open Flash by selecting Flash File ActionScript 3.0 and on the left side in tool panel select Text Tool or press quick key T.

2. Place cursor on left side in the middle of rectangle shaped white stage and type upper case C, as shown in picture 1.4

Picture 1.4

3. After you type, click the first tool at the top left which is Selection Tool or press quick key V. Go down to Property and increase its font size to 70.

4. Now click under the Frame 5 in timeline at the top and press F6 to insert a dot. Take Text tool again and type lower case r. With the help of selection tool place it next to capital C as shown in picture 1.5

Picture 1.5

5. Click back on Frame 1 in timeline having Selection Tool active with mouse pointer. When you see that a red line has come on Frame 1 which means you are on Frame 1 where your capital C is, go to property panel.

6. In the dropdown of Tween, select Motion. Do not select Shape this time as it will not work and Flash will show an error with pink exclamation mark next to Tween option and a dash in timeline, which means Flash detected your mistake.

7. Now press enter to see the small part of this animation. You see that first the letter c and then r comes in animated on the screen. Right now it is quite small, but don't worry, there a little more to do with this.

8. As you typed letter r, click on Frame 10, press F6 and type the next letter o. Place it next to previous one and then apply same Motion effect.

9. Like this, type the other letters m, o, s, y, s one after another giving them the space of five frames each in the timeline, which means type m at Frame 15, o at Frame 20, s at Frame 25 and so on. Give Motion effect to all of them and your screen will look like as shown in picture 1.6

10. Do not commit any mistake while doing this especially in clicking on frames and inserting dot by pressing F6. Even a single mistake will mess up the entire animation and you have will have to start all allover again as Flash is very unforgiving in this. Do not use copy-paste shortcut but type each letter on the stage.

11. After you apply Motion effect to all, press enter to see the animation.

How Animation Works

Animation is made from individual images. Regardless of how motion is created in an animation, an animation is still a collection of fixed (still) images. When you watch a movie or television, the screen is blinking very fast – sometimes it shows an image, and other time it is blank. The fact that the blank moments are so short that you think you're watching full motion but you watch only still images.

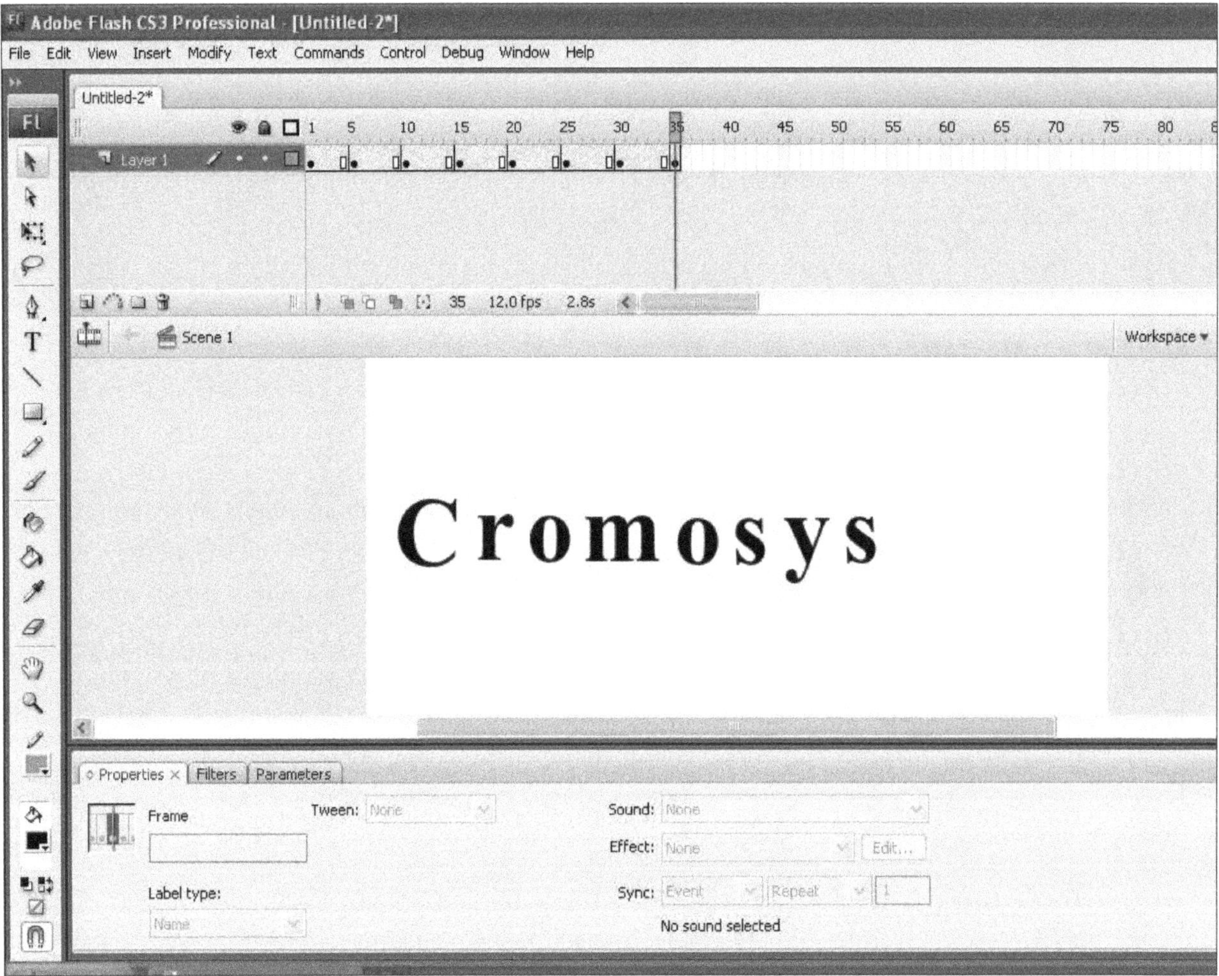

Picture 1.6

Now we are takings steps ahead to understand more functions of Flash. Don't forget to practice over these two lessons before moving ahead.

Lesson 3
Make a Frame-by-Frame Animation

In this task you're going to make an animation of a stick man talking a walk on the screen. Follow these steps:

1. Draw a stick man by using only lines (no fills) and make sure everything is snapped together, as shown in picture 1.7. While drawing, you may have to turn off Fill-color option under Color Tab of top right panel, as shown in picture 1.7.

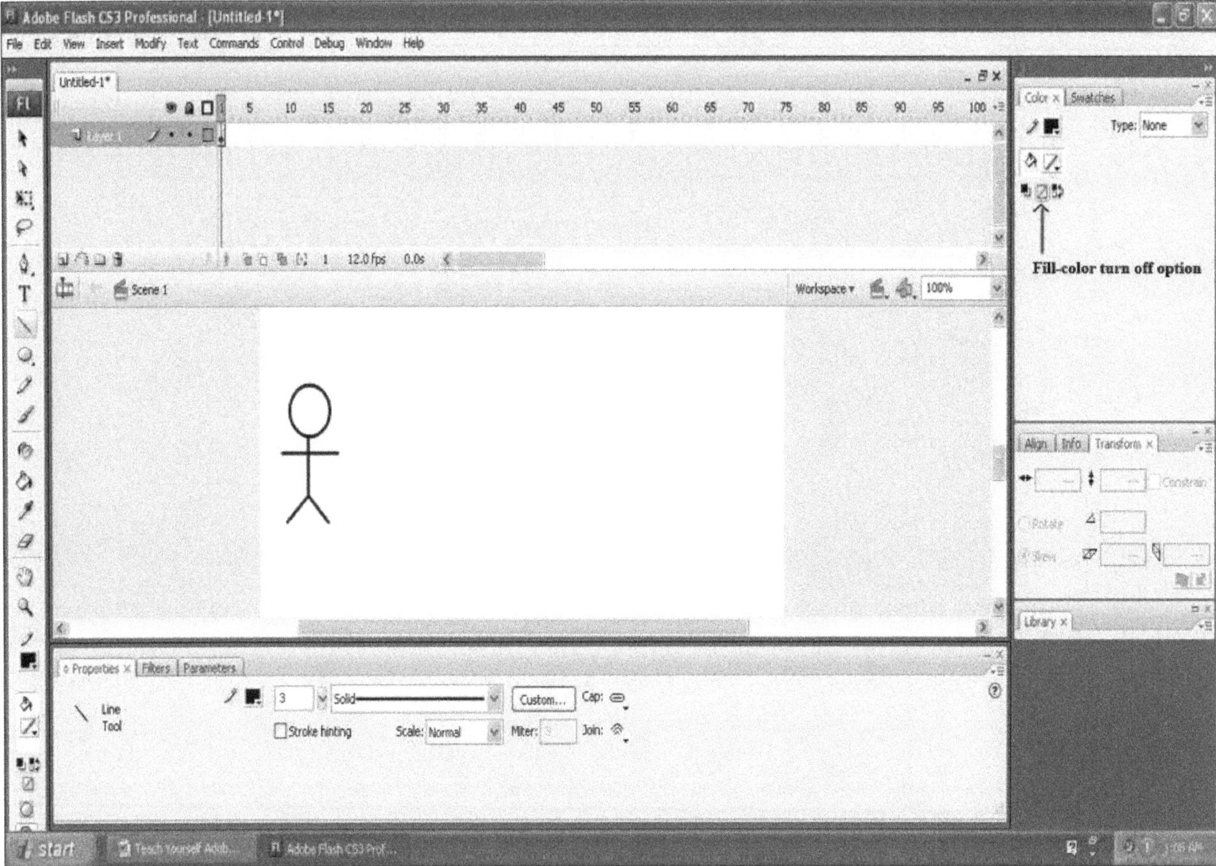

Picture 1.7

2. Single click on Frame 2 and insert a keyframe by pressing F6 or going to Insert, Timeline, Keyframe.

3. The stickman gets automatically copied to keyframe 2. You are going to edit Frame 2 and you will see that in Timeline the red current-frame marker is in Frame 2. If it is not there, click in Frame 2 of the Timeline.

4. Now you're going to make a slight change to the stickman's leg. The moment you insert dot in Frame 2, the stickman gets copied. Click on Selection Tool, click once outside stickman to deselect its entire body. Now placing pointer on its leg with the Selection Tool active, bend its one leg slightly and change the end point of the arm so it looks like it's swinging (as in picture 1.8).

5. Press enter and you'll see how stickman begins to take a step. Now create a third Frame by clicking on Frame 3 and insert keyframe. Make some more changes to its leg and arm.

6. Continue to insert keyframes, one at a time. Make an edit to each new Frame to keep the arms and legs moving. Finally press Ctrl + Enter to see it in movie.

The concept behind the frame-by-frame animation technique is simple. You just put a keyframe on each Frame. An entirely different image appears on each Frame. The beauty is that you can put anything you want in one keyframe because it doesn't matter what's in the other keyframes.

Picture 1.8

The Frame-by-Frame Animation is the simple conventional technique, however there are advanced options associated with this technique that you're going to learn in next lesson. Don't give up, just keep moving.

Lesson 4
Implying Motion

In this lesson you're going to make a movie of the two stickmen playing football. In this, first stickman will kick the ball and it will go to right side's stickman. Here you don't need to draw each step while the ball moves toward right side but itself does it for you. Only you have to draw starting and ending point. This two-frame theory is called Implying Motion. While doing this, you'll learn some more features of Flash like Changing Frame view setting, Onion Skin, and Pause.

1. Draw a stickman in Frame 1 with a ball near his foot as shown in picture 1.9.

2. Insert keyframe in frame 5 and bend his leg to look like he going to kick the ball.

3. Insert keyframe in Frame 10, click on the ball (only ball) with your Selection Tool to select and then drag it to the middle of the stage to look like it has been kicked.

4. Now insert keyframe in Frame 15, with Selection Tool drag the ball to right side of the stage. In Frame 20, give a pause by inserting keyframe and don't make any change in drawing to make it look more natural to convince that the ball stops there for a second.

5. In Frame 25, select the entire stickman by dragging over it with Selection Tool and then move it to right side near the ball to show it as second stickman.

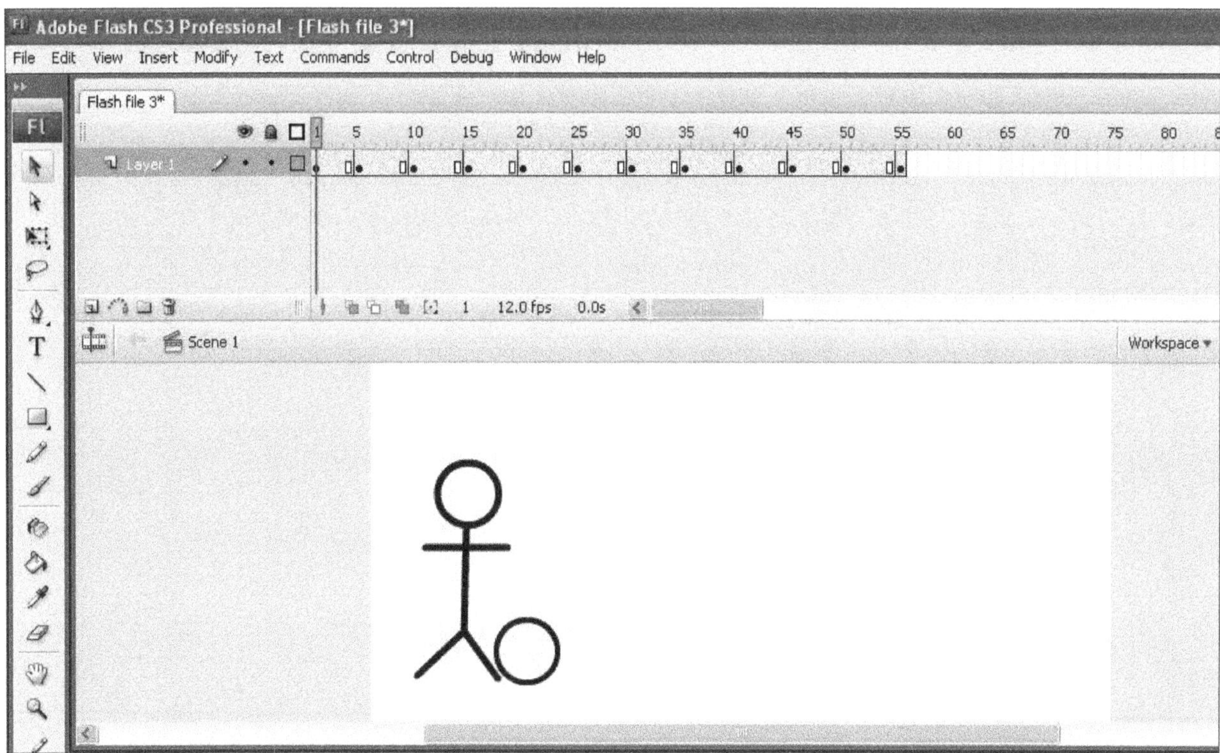

Picture 1.9

Picture 2.0 shows all the three drawings that you've done till now.

Picture 2.0

6. In Frame 30 give a pause again. In Frame 35, bend second stickman's leg to kick the ball and this way keep on adding keyframes doing small changes in drawing to make it look like the two stickmen are playing football.

To make Implying Motion steps easier, Flash facilitates Frame View setting which allows you to see the small icon of each drawing in the timeline. To access that you can click on Frame view drop-down menu this is at the far end of the timeline as shown in picture 2.1. Select Preview from the drop-down. To go back to the previous setting you can click on Small.

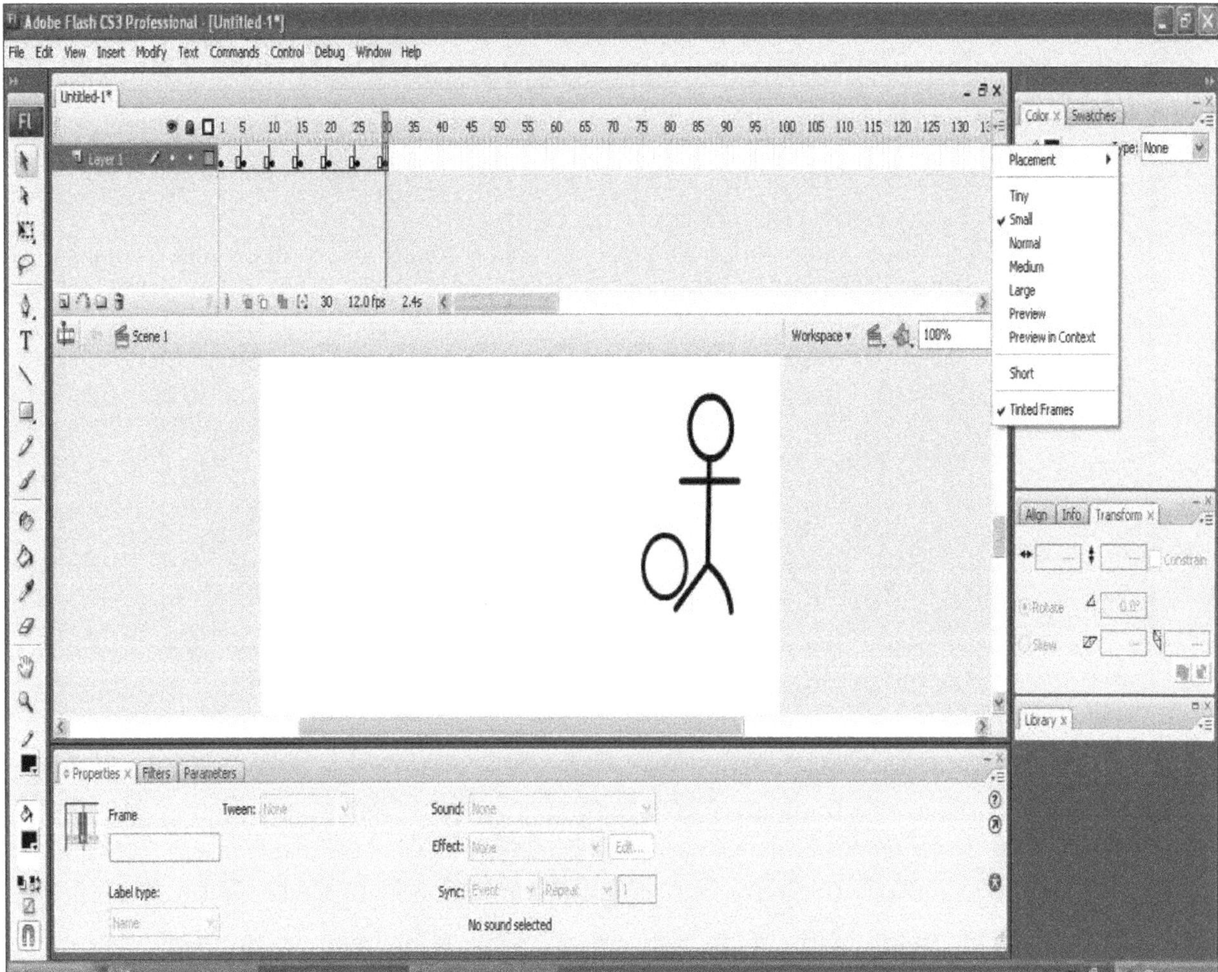

Picture 2.1

There is one more thing that you can take benefit of while working one Implying Motion, and that is Onion Skin tool. Once this tool is activated (as shown in picture 2.2), if you're drawing at a particular Frame, you can see the previous Frame's drawing also, and that helps you to be certain in drawing. You can turn on and off this tool as per your requirement.

The picture 2.2 shows how you'll activate Onion Skin tool.

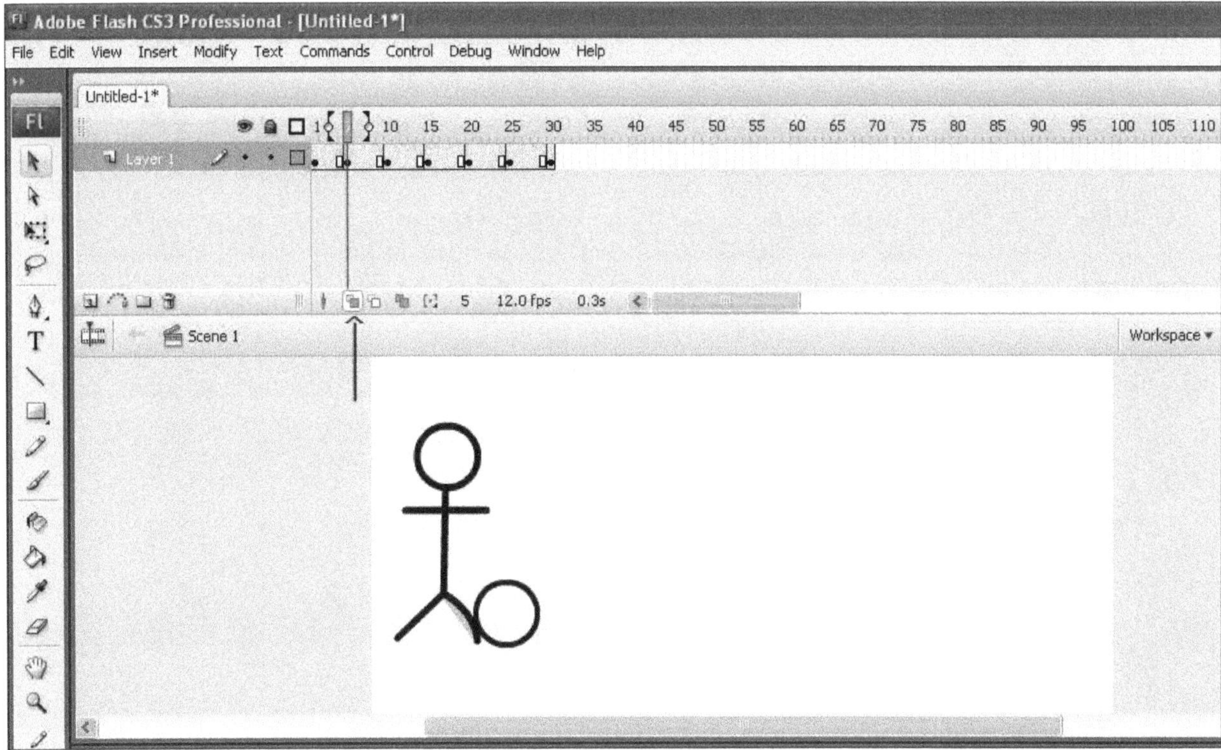

Picture 2.2

Picture 2.3
Having Onion Skin on you can see the drawing of previous Frame while working on next.

Lesson 5
Basic Motion Tween

In this lesson you'll make a circle animate across the screen by using the Motion Tween feature:

1. Open a new file and draw a circle on the left side of stage as shown in picture 2.4.

2. Select the entire circle using Selection Tool and click Modify, Convert to Symbol (or press F8), Name it Circle, leave other option as it is and click OK. Once you save an instance (any drawing) in library by converting to symbol, you can use it as many times but it won't increase the size of movie. To access Library, you can click on Windows, Library.

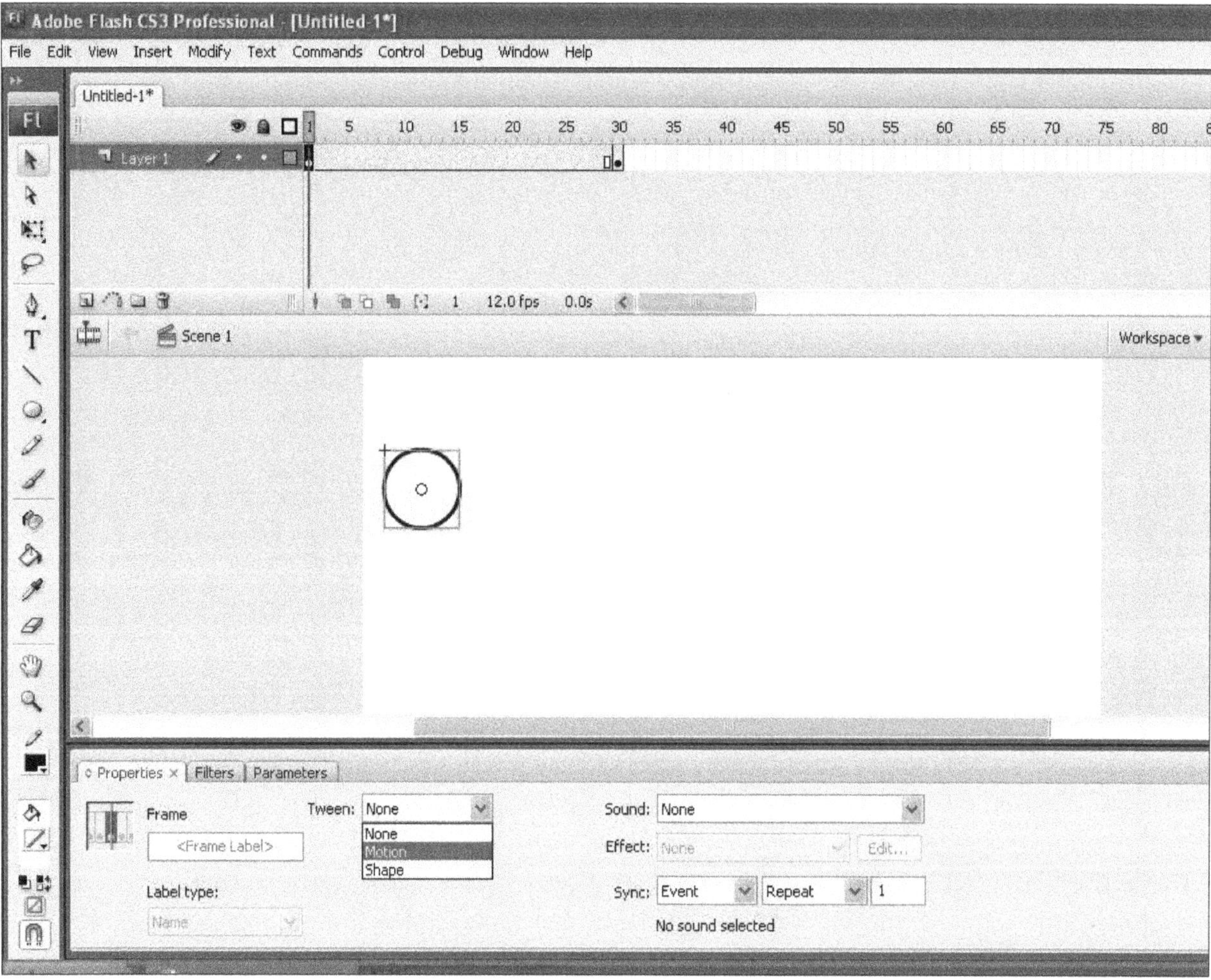

Picture 2.4

3. Click Frame 30 in the Timeline and insert a keyframe, and then drag the circle to place on the right side of stage.

4. Click on the keyframe in Frame 1. If you press enter to see, the circle stays on the left side for 29 frames and then jumps to the right side. This is exactly where you need tweening to have Flash take care of the in-between frames.

5. When you have keyframe in Frame 1 selected, go to Properties panel and select Motion in Tween drop-down list as shown in picture 2.4.

6. Flash will have an arrow in the Timeline to represent the interpolated frames. Press Ctrl + Enter to see what happens.

Remember that Motion Tween doesn't work when you have multiple objects in the keyframes. And an object (called instance in Flash) must be converted to symbol before applying Motion Tween. And in case of Shape Tween, you don't need to group anything or convert an object to symbol. Avoid these common mistakes while working in Flash.

Lesson 6
Fine-Tune Animation

Now you're going to create a Fine-Tune Animation. From this lesson onwards you'll start realizing how the significance of your own creation.

1. Open a new file and draw a small circle in the middle with no fill-color in it. Just the line color should be black as shown in picture 2.5.

2. While drawing, if you find your circle not coming in round shape, use Selection Tool to curve and put in right shape.

3. Click on Frame 2 and insert a keyframe in it. Change the line color from the option of right panel and draw another circle over black one that you already have. Make sure that this one should be different in color and bigger in size over previous one as shown in the same picture 2.5.

4. Insert keyframe in Frame 3 but don't make any change on stage as it is going to be a pause in your animation.

5. Insert keyframe in Frame 4, change the line color and draw another circle (third one) over previous one bigger in size.

6. Like this, draw at least 8 circles of different colors giving pause after 3 keyframes.

7. When all the 8 circles are drawn, give a pause again by inserting a blank keyframe in the next Frame.

8. Press Ctrl + Enter to see your amazing creation.

9. When you want to save this file, keep that in mind that saving it in .fla format will let you edit the same file later also. If you save it in .swf format, you can play your animation in a continuous loop in Flash Player which is already installed in your system with Flash software. And if you save it in .avi format, you would be able to play it in Windows and third party media player.

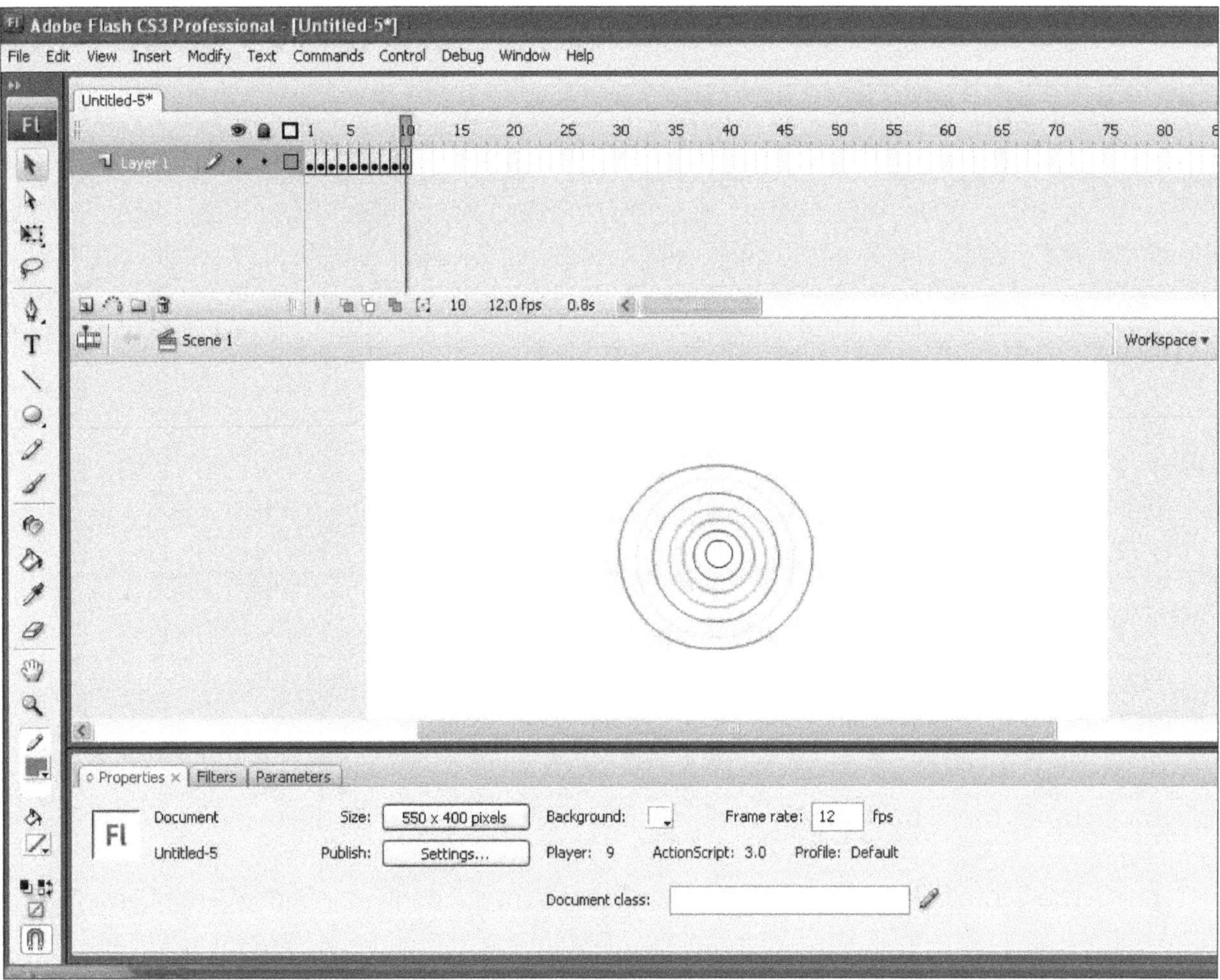

Picture 2.5

This Fine-Tune animation doesn't require any Tween effect, but if you want to know what difference the Shape Tween can make in this drawing, then follow these steps.

1. Open a new file and draw a small circle of black color in the middle with no fill-color in it.

2. Insert a keyframe in Frame 30 and draw a bigger circle over black one of a different color. You can change the width of the line as per your choice or leave it as it is. For that you can go to Properties Panel.

3. Select keyframe 1 and apply Shape effect Tween dropdown. Press Ctrl + Enter to see what happens.

Lesson 7
Simple Shape Tween

Now here is what you'd be waiting for! This animation is definitely going to amaze you. You're going to create a Shape-Tween animation which will enliven your drawing on stage. In this lesson you'll draw a shape and then cut it half which is technically called Morphing.

1. In a new file, draw a circle of red color on the stage. Make sure that this time line-color on the right panel should be turned off, and don't group anything or convert anything to symbol. Picture 2.6 shows you how your circle looks like.

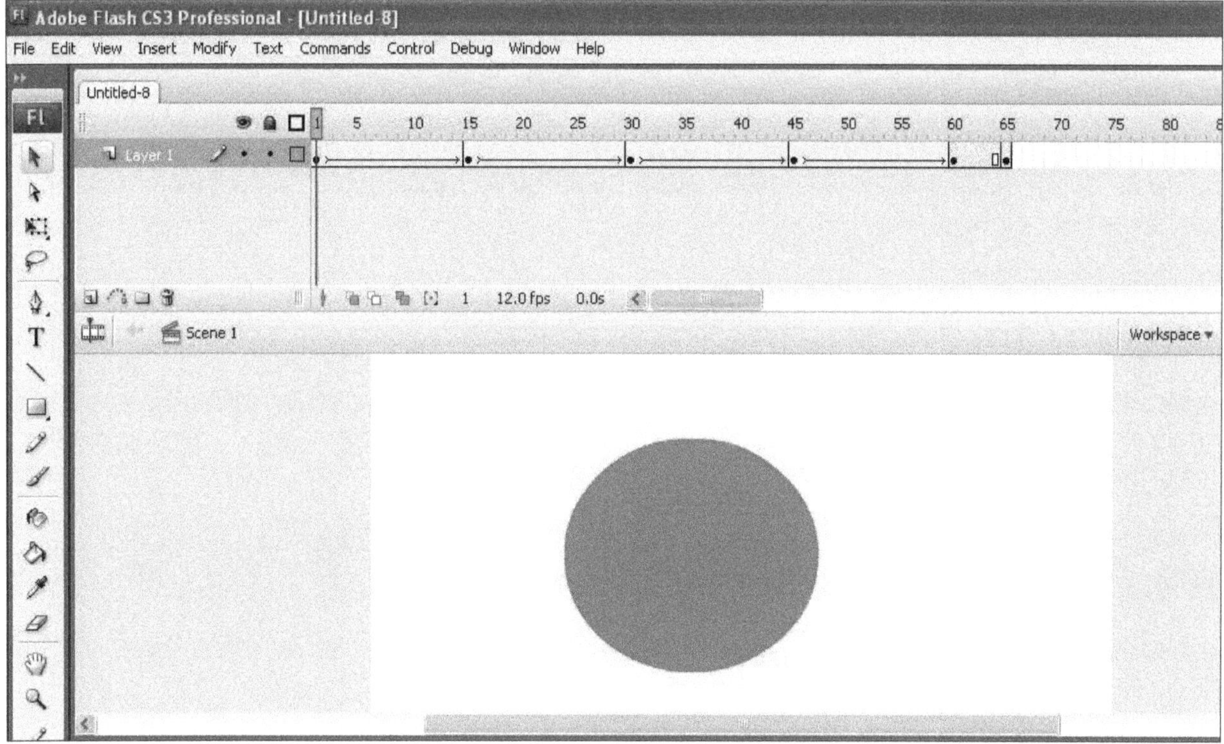

Picture 2.6

2. Insert keyframe in Frame 30 by pressing F6.

3. Insert keyframe in Frame 15. Click on Selection Tool and click off the circle on stage to deselect it. Now bring the pointer close to the edge until the cursor changes to a curved-tail pointer. Click and drag toward the center of the circle to reshape it in half, as shown in picture 2.7.

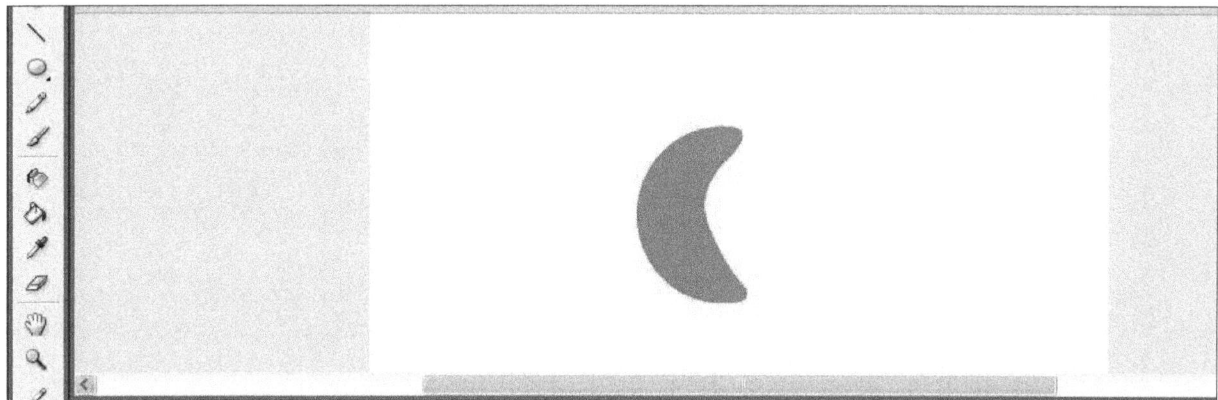

Picture 2.7

4. Now you'll set tweening for the two snaps. First click Frame 1 and while holding Shift key down click Frame 15. In the Properties panel, select Shape from the Tween dropdown list.

5. Press Ctrl + Enter to see your animation. You can add some more keyframes after Frame 30, and with your imagination, you can give a different shape to the circle from left side also which will make it look like a flying-bird. You can give a pause at the end to make it look better in loop play.

Lesson 8
Tween Position, Scale, Rotation, and Color

1. In a new file, type your name using Text tool. You need not worry about the size, but make it big enough to see clearly.

2. Using the Selection tool select the text block (not the text itself). Then convert it to symbol by pressing shortcut key F8, name the symbol My Name and click OK.

3. Insert a keyframe in Frame 30 and click outside the text block on the stage. Now click on Frame 1 and when red current-frame marker comes on it, position your name in the bottom-left corner which is the initial position of the text.

4. While the first keyframe is selected, choose Motion from the Tween dropdown list in the Properties panel.

5. Click on Frame 30 to edit its end position. Select the Free Transform tool (or press Q) and make it large enough to occupy the entire stage.

6. You can press enter to see how it is going to look like or scrub it by pressing and dragging your mouse pointer from Frame 30 to Frame 1. Remember that in this animation you can only edit the properties for the instance in either the beginning or ending keyframe, not between.

7. Now select Frame 30 and modify the color effect of this symbol. To do this, select this instance, go to Properties and select Tint in the Color Style dropdown list as shown in picture 2.8.

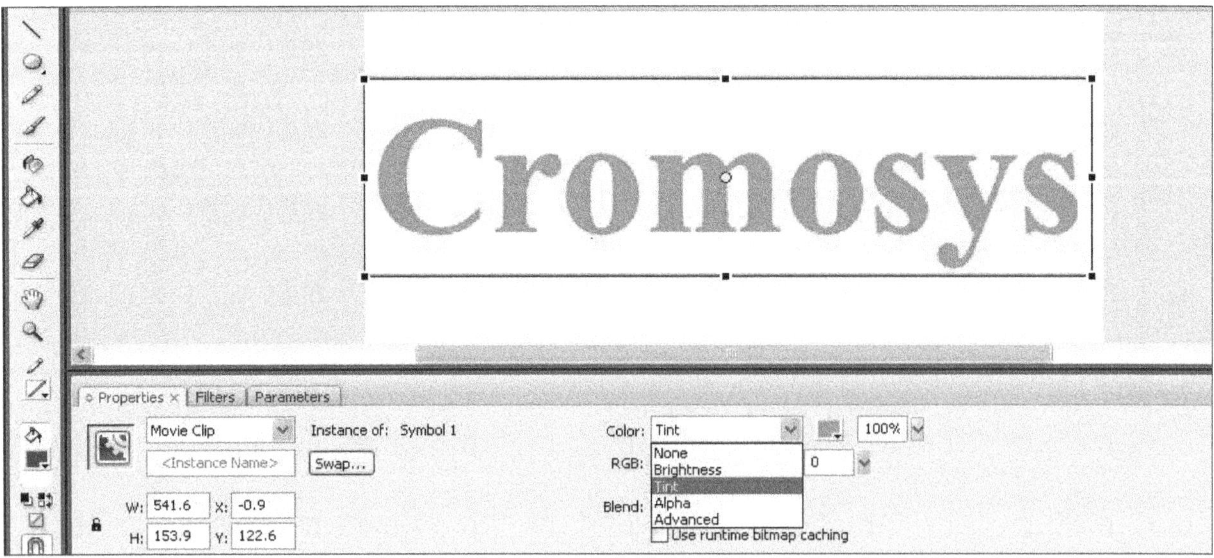

Picture 2.8

8. After you pick a different color, set the percentage to 100% and press enter to see the change.

9. Go to Frame 1 and with the Free Transform tool, rotate your name counter-clock wise just a few degree, as shown in picture 2.9. Do a little skewing, too. When the Rotate option for the Transform tool is selected, the corner handles rotate and middle handles skew.

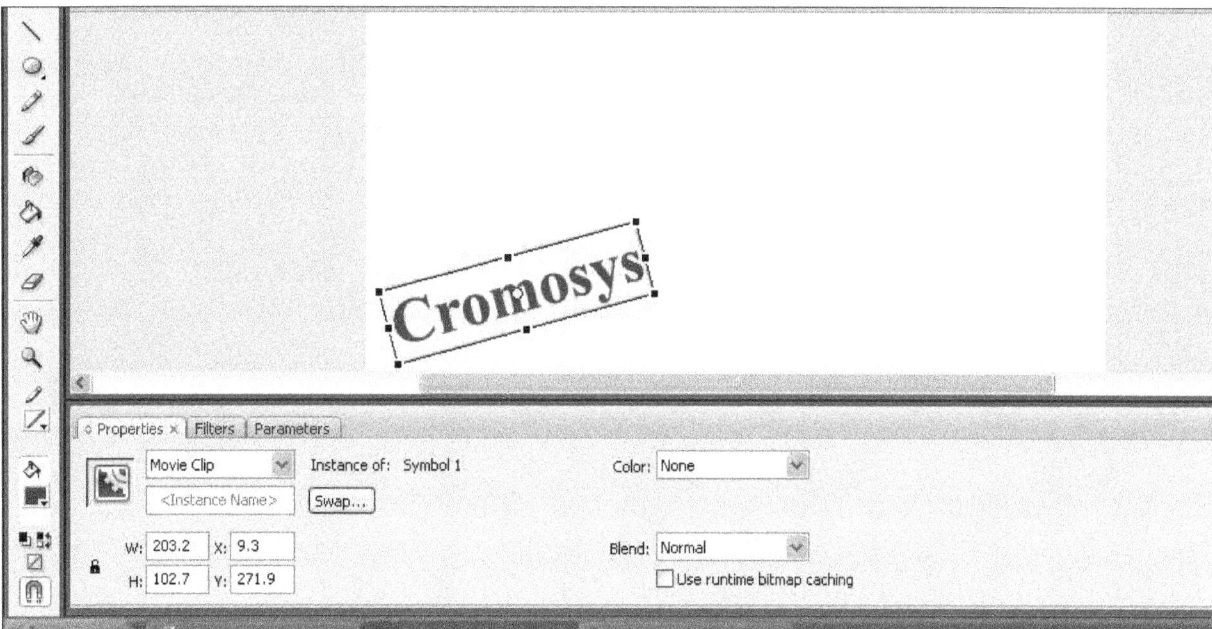

Picture 2.9

10. Check out your animation by scrubbing or testing your movie. You've created two very different keyframes, and Flash figured out how to animate from one to another.

Things to remember
Although Shape Tween and Motion Tween can always help you create an animation, but sometimes the most effective animation is the most subtle. That means sometimes the best solution is frame-by-frame animation, such as what you did in lesson 4. Frame-by-frame animation takes more time but it is more stable.

Lesson 9
Ease In and Ease Out

When you apply tween effect to your animation, Flash makes it look like too much computerized. In another word, it looks like a machine did it. So to give your animation an apparent human touch, Flash has Easing tool which brings acceleration or deceleration to the motion of tweening you set. However, you can apply only one setting per tween between two keyframes.

1. In a new file, draw any shape and select it entirely by dragging Selection Tool pointer over it. Now make it a symbol by pressing F8 and name it as you want. After that, place the symbol somewhere on the left side of the stage.

2. Click Frame 50 in the Timeline and insert a keyframe by pressing F6. While the red current-frame is in Frame 50, move the instance of the symbol to the right side of the stage.

3. Click Frame 100 and move the instance of the symbol to the left side where it was initially. Now we have two set of keyframes, first from Frame 1 to 50 and second from Frame 50 to 100. To apply Easing, you need two set of keyframes.

4. Go back to Frame 1 and create a motion tween from Properties panel. You can use a shortcut by right-clicking and selecting Create Motion Tween also. Select Frame 50 also and apply the same effect.

5. Press Ctrl + Enter to test the movie and remember how it looks. It would be moving on the screen with a fixed speed.

6. Now we'll use Easing tool. Click on Frame 1 and click on the Ease slider down below the Tween option as shown in the picture 3.0. Sliding it up is called Ease in which means that the motion starts off slow and speeds up at the end. Sliding it down is called Ease out which is the opposite – the object starts by going fast and then slows down at the end.

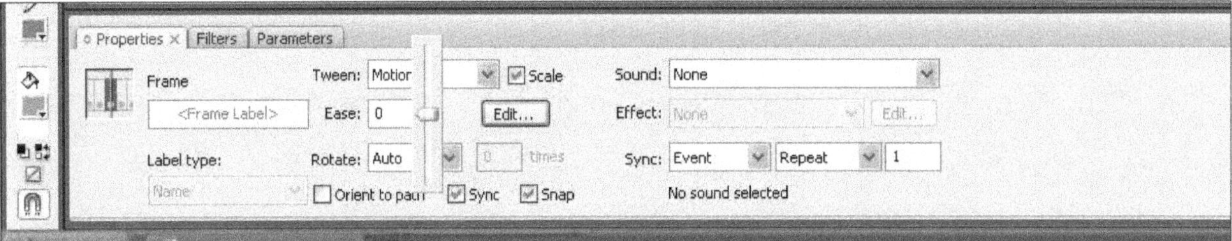

Picture 3.0

7. As Frame 1 is already clicked, now move the slider up to the top. Then (don't play the movie – just wiat) click on Frame 50 and move the slider down to the bottom. Ease in and Ease out effect go together so don't try to play the movie just after applying one effect.

8. Now press Ctrl + Enter and you'll notice the movement of the animation is changed as explained above.

9. Now we'll use custom editing tool. For that, click on Frame 1 and then click the Edit button adjacent to the Easing slider as shown in picture 3.1. The graph area displays a line to show how much of the tween has completed over time.

10. You can click on the graph line and the control points let you modify the shape of graph the way you want which would affect the animation on stage. You can play preview also while making change in it.

11. After you're done with that, click OK on the graph and test the movie to watch how it behaves. I'm sure this time it looks more fascinating to you.

12. In addition to that, if you want, you can rotate the instance on stage also. For that, select Frame 1, click on Rotate dropdown, select CW and put 3 in times box.

13. Play the movie again and I won't ask how much you love your animation now!

The graph area displays a line to show how much of the tween has completed over time.

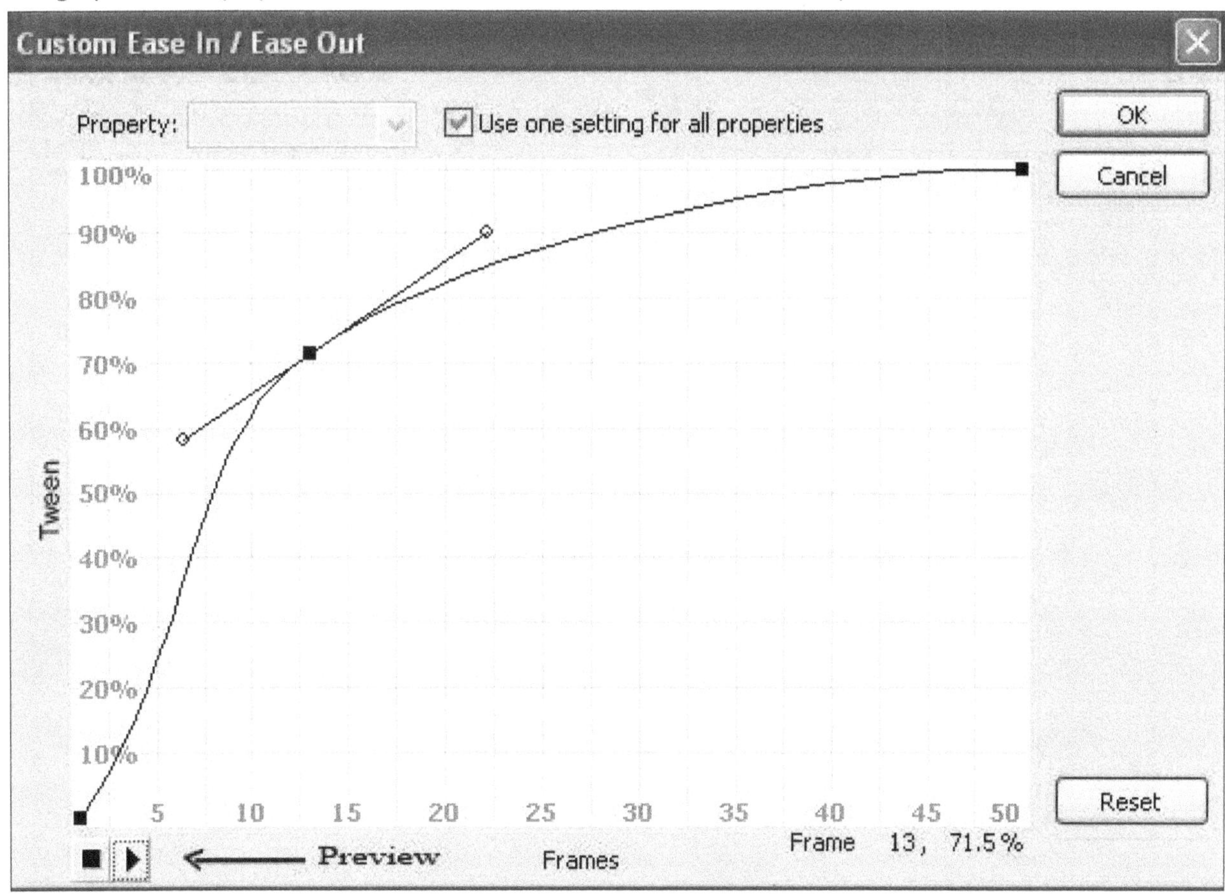

Picture 3.1

Lesson 10
Editing Interpolated Keyframes

In this lesson we're going to edit interpolated frames which are fixed keyframes between two frames. You've to be careful while making any change in the interpolation because that is what you're responsible of in terms of the result.

1. Draw a sky-blue color rectangle of medium size and place it in the top-middle of the stage.

2. Insert keyframe in Frame 10, deselect the rectangle by clicking off of it, and then select dark blue color. After every instance you need to deselect so that the color change can affect next object only.

3. Draw an oval in dark blue color and place it below the rectangle as shown in picture 3.2.

4. Insert keyframe in Frame 20, deselect the oval and select black color now.

5. Select brush from Tool panel and draw an L shape object below the oval. Though you can type L from keyboard also but remember that Flash doesn't accept Shape effect done on text if it is too weird to its accompanied object.

6. Insert keyframe in Frame 25 to give a pause only. Now hold shift and select keyframe 1 and 10 and create Shape Tween effect. Test the movie after it is done. It's cool, isn't it?

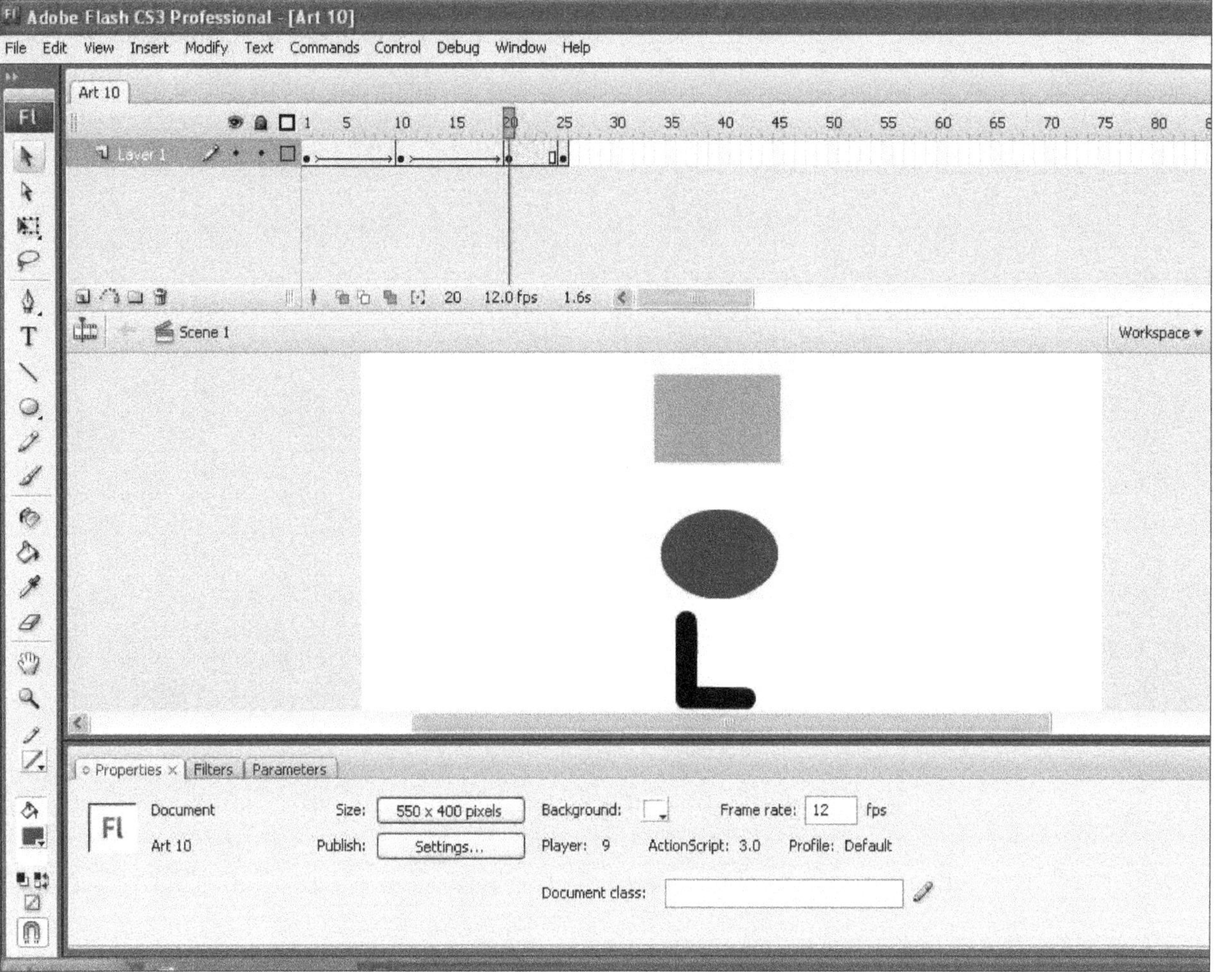

Picture 3.2

Things to remember
The reason to use brush while drawing L was that Shape Tween easily accepts brush-drawn shape. If you type L, you might not get Shape Tween giving expected result because it doesn't work in weird situation. One more thing to remember is that if you apply Motion Tween (not in this animation, but some other), the letter you type has to be converted to symbol. And in case you type a word of two letters, you have to select both letters and break them apart by going to Modify>Break Apart, and then you have to convert both of these letters to shape separately. Sorry, there is no other way!

7. Now we're going to edit interpolated keyframes to animate in our way. For this, you need to click somewhere between 1 and 10 Frames on the Shape Tween arrow. If you press F5 on this, it will add hidden keyframes and increase the length of animation, and holding shift and pressing F5 work opposite. But to edit interpolation you have press F6 which will add a dot with keyframe.

8. Pick up the Selection Too and move the oval toward right by dragging. Now play the movie and see how it looks.

Lesson 11
Using Shape Hints

In this lesson you'll use Shape Hints feature to crate a better Shape Tween.

1. In a new file, select the Rectangle tool and ensure Object Drawing option at the far bottom of the tool panel is turned off. Object Drawing option is shown in picture 3.3.

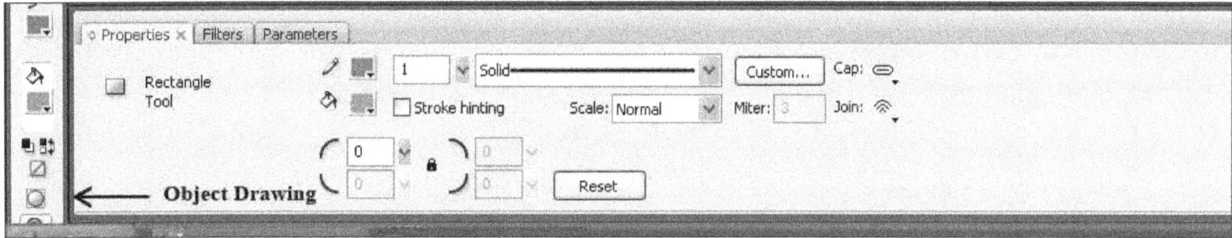

Picture 3.3

2. Draw a perfect square by using the Rectangle tool holding shift key down.

3. Enable Frame 25 by pressing F6, and change the square to rectangle. Don't worry; there are many ways to do this. Here are the sub-steps to change the square to rectangle.

(A) When you are in Frame 25, use Sub-selection tool while having Onion Skin on.
(B) Or, in Frame 25, draw a vertical line that doesn't touch the square. Take Selection tool, make sure Snap to Objects option is turned ON under View>Snapping. Now click once on the line to select it, and click and hold in the end of the line. When you click and hold the line, you get a solid circle at the bottom of the line indicating that you have grabbed the end. If you fail once, try it again. Picture 3.4 shows how it would look like.

Picture 3.4

(C) As you've grabbed the line, now drag it to snap in the center of the horizontal top of the square as shown in picture 3.5. Then grab the top-left corner of the square (without clicking on it to select), and drag it until it snaps to the bisecting line to be a triangle. Picture 3.5 also shows a solid circle when you grab the square.

(D) After you do that, it should look as shown in picture 3.6.

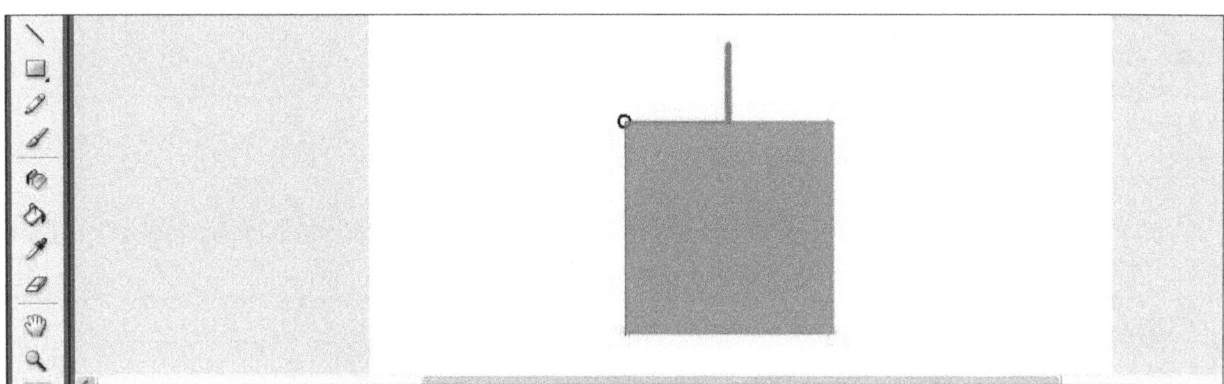

Picture 3.5

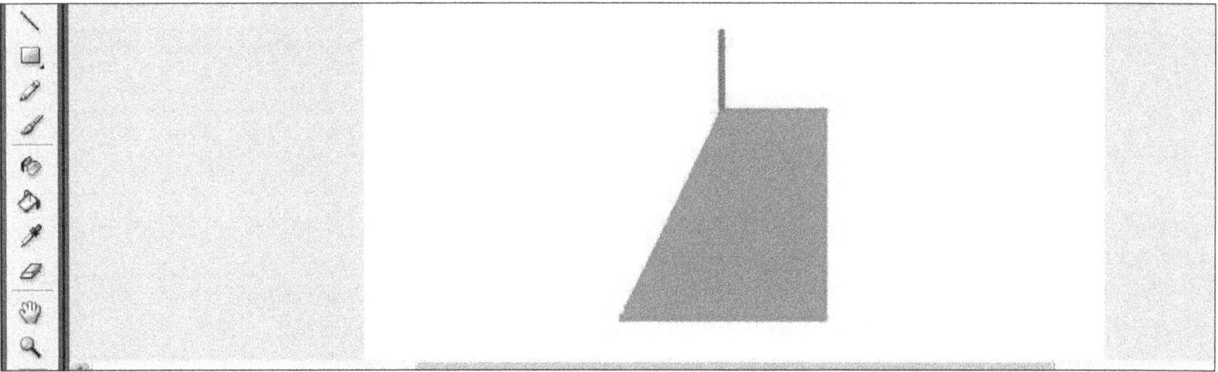

Picture 3.6

(E) Do the same for the top-right corner of the square. Then delete the vertical line and it would look as shown in picture 3.7.

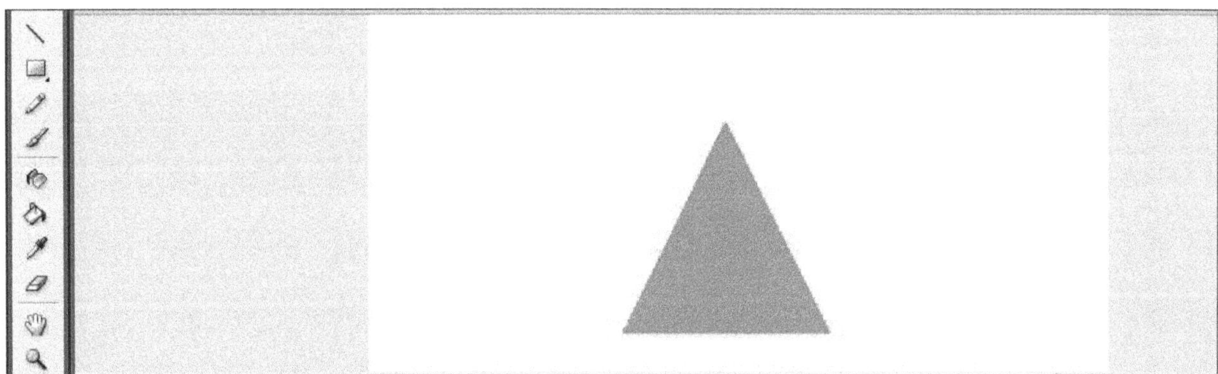

Picture 3.7

4. Select the keyframe 1 and apply Shape Tween effect. Press enter to play and you'll see that the result is not good as because the square rotates as it tweens to the triangle. Now is your chance to use the Shape Hints feature.

5. Under the View menu, ensure that Show Shape Hints has a check mark (select if it is not).

6. Go to Frame 1 and select Modify> Shape> Add Shape Hint (or press Ctrl+Shift+H).

7. Notice a little red circle with the letter a (a shape hint). Temporarily move the red current-frame marker to Frame 25 and notice that there's also an a shape hint in this frame.

8. Make sure you're back in Frame 1 and that Snap to Object is still turned ON (or select by going to View> Snapping> Snap to Objects). Using Selection tool you can drag the shape hint to the top-left corner of the square as shown in picture 3.8. It is in red color which indicates that you haven't mapped this point to an end point yet.

Picture 3.8

9. Go to Frame 25 and position Shape Hint so that it snaps to the middle of the left side of the triangle. Notice that the shape hint turns green which indicates that it's been mapped. Also, when you return to Frame 1, the shape hint is colored yellow to indicate that it's been mapped, as shown in picture 3.9.

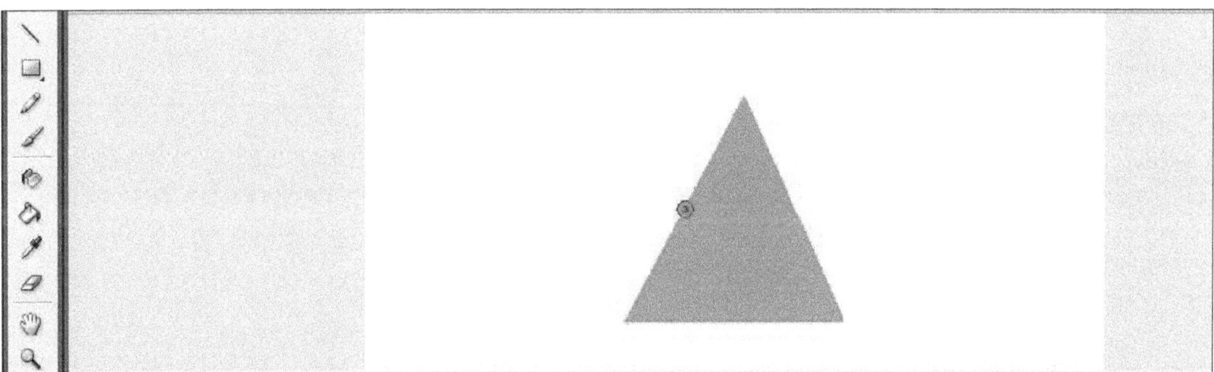

Picture 3.9

10. Press enter to see the animation. If it looks good, you don't need to add any more shape hints. If you think the square, on the right side does animate properly, then you've to add one more shape hint.

12. In Frame 1, add one more shape hint following the same step which comes as b. Position it in the top-right corner of the square. In Frame 25, map Shape Hint b to snap to the middle of the right side of the triangle.

13. Now don't add any more shape hints. Test the movie to see the result.

Tips for Shape Hints
It can be used only with a pair of keyframes. Don't use more Shape Hints than necessary. By adding it, you tell Flash that this point in the starting shape goes with that point in the ending shape.

You can add Shape Hint only when you're in first keyframe with shape tweening already set. To see the invisible hints you can always go to View> Show Shape Hints, and to remove it by right-clicking or Modify> Shape> Remove All Hints.

Lesson 12
Understanding Frame Rate

We are going to create one more frame-by-frame animation in which you have to draw on every frame. Here let me tell you something about frame rate as well. In the properties panel you see an option that says Frame rate 12/fps. That means in one second it will play 12 frames, and if you have an animation of 60 frames, it will take 4 seconds to play. Right now you don't need to change the frame rate.

1. Open a new file and draw a face in Frame 1 as shown in picture 4.0. You can use Selection tool to move, copy and paste the object. You can use zoom tool while drawing the eyeballs.

Picture 4.0

2. Now if you press F6, it automatically enables the very next keyframe. So keep pressing for inserting new keyframes and at every keyfreame make some change on this face. The changes can be like the eyeball rolling up and down and the mouth-line drawn down to smile.

3. After inserting at least 25 keyframes with changes done on each one of them, finally on Frame 25 it should look like a smiley face as shown in picture 4.1.

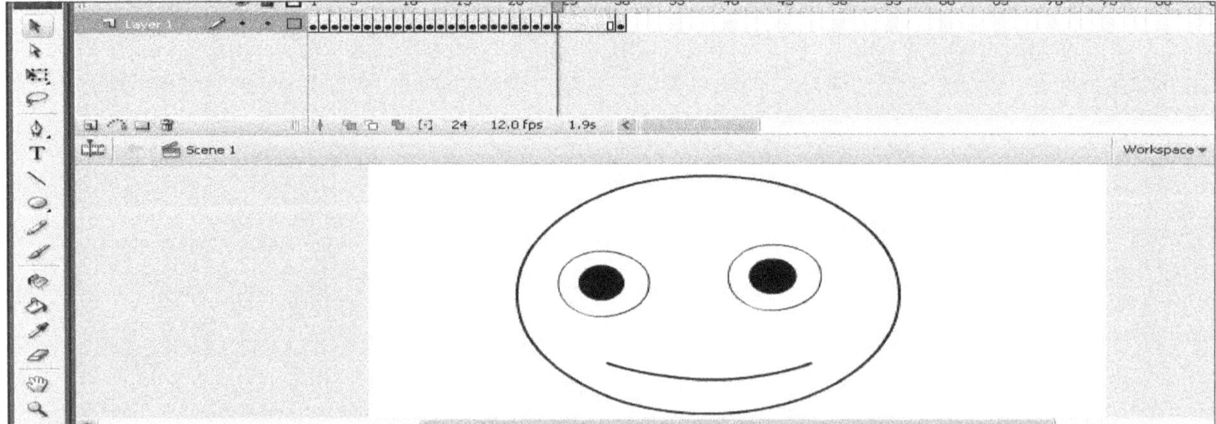

Picture 4.1

4. Give a pause at Frame 35 and play the movie to see how it looks.

To understand the frame rate, it is clear here that this animation of 35 keyfames can be played in about 3 seconds of time. In this dynamic animation, Shape or Motion Tween will not work.

Lesson 13
Importing Graphic and Sound

You can import graphics and sounds in Flash. For graphics, JPEG or even .psd (Photoshop) format works great. For sounds, Flash has great support but it has no internal way to record or create sound. For this, either you can record sound using Sound Recorder of Windows operating system or any third party software. Even many of the musical instruments have the facility to record sound. Flash supports MP3, WAV, AIF, and AU audio formats. You can even download audio files of your choice from Internet as well. Though Flash has the tools to resize your sound to fit the drawing, but it should not be too long then required. In that case you can use Windows Movie Maker to cut your sound, but after you save the file in .wma format, you have to covert it back to the above mentioned format using online converters. But be careful as any glitch in audio file can get it stuck.

In order to import graphics or sounds, you must import them to Flash's Library – not anywhere else. Now in this lesson we're going to create an animation using sound.

1. In a new file, select File> Import> Import to Library and then select the audio file. After you select, you can click OK in the dialog box. To see it in Library (which you may not need), you can click on Windows> Library.

2. Now you can start your drawing with a black rectangle touching the bottom part of the stage as shown in picture 4.2. In this dynamic animation you can change the Timeline and Stage view as per your convenience from the dropdown shown in the picture.

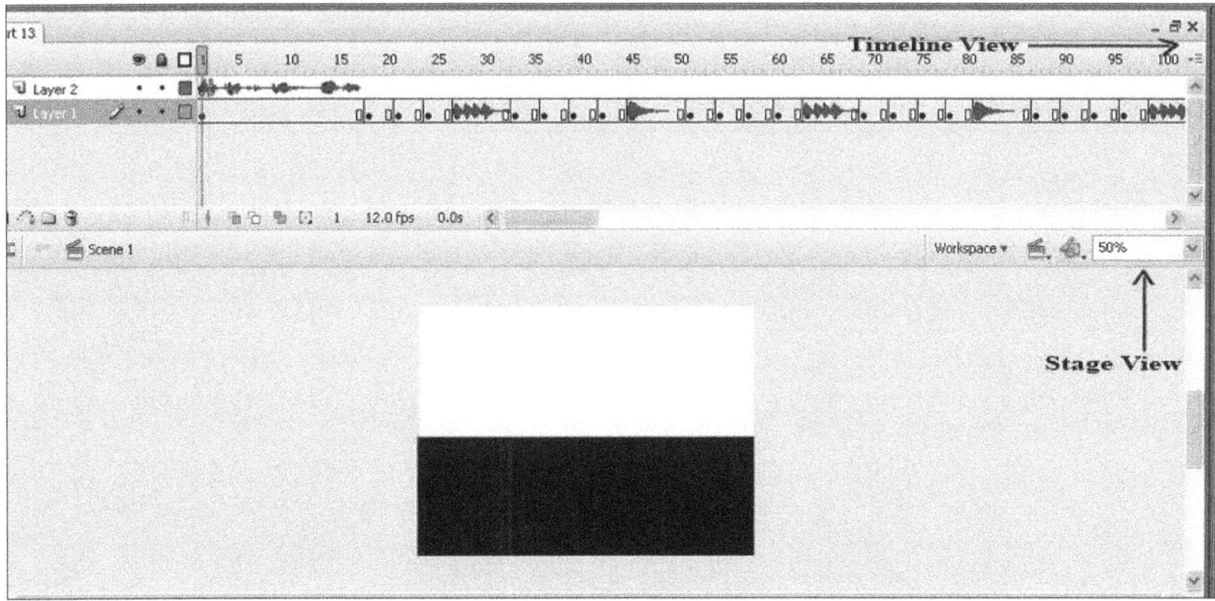

Picture 4.2

3. Go three frames ahead, for which, you can use F5 and then press F6. Pressing F5 lets you selection point in the Timeline move ahead and Shift + F5 takes it back. After enabling the keyframe type the letter F and covert it to symbol. Rememer that each letter of this drawing has to be converted to symbol.

4. You can place it in small size at the top and adding keyframes after every three frames you can let it come down on black rectangle growing in size. Keep that in mind that it is going to be your frame-by-frame animation, so don't think of Shape or Motion Tween. Here you can show your own art.

5. The Onion Skin will help you putting the symbol at right place. You can see the exact location of each instance from Properties panel also, which can be used in case you're lost somewhere at the finishing point.

6. Giving a distance of three keyframes you should have the word FLASH on your stage probably as it looks on my screen in picture 4.3.

Picture 4.3

7. Create a new layer for audio by right-clicking on the existing drawing layer. You'll see a new layer in the Timeline. Now click on the keyframe of the drawing layer where you want to insert audio, and in the Properties, click on Sound dropdown and select the audio file.

8. Pressing Enter will let you hear the sound. Now you'll enter the gigantic setting of audio.

9. You can click on Edit option which is next to Effect button. The Time In and Time Out Marker will let you trim the sound. It works as a Start and End Timer without cutting your original file in Library. You can cut the silence in the beginning of your audio using this so that your file size remains small. Picture 4.4 shows the Effect option. Audio file is also an electronic data so don't put too many sounds in your animation. That's it, play the movie to see the result!

Here I am giving you some information about the Synch option which you find below Effect.
Event – This option should be your default choice because if Event is chosen, it will start to play when the keyframe is reached and keep playing until the sound is done.
Start – This setting is almost the same as Event, except that multiple instances of the same sound are prevented.
Stop – It is for when you want a specified sound to stop playing.
Stream – This setting causes the sound to remain perfectly synchronized with the Timeline.

Picture 4.4

The additional details of the Effect settings
Left Channel/Right Channel – This option displays different wave forms if your original sound is stereo.
Envelope lines – These indicates the volume level at any particular time in the sound. You can increase of decrease the sound using these Envelope lines. On these lines, you can add handles anywhere by double-clicking and then drag them down or up.
Time In Marker – It lets you establish the starting point of a sound.
Time Out Marker – This marker lets you trim extra sound off the end of a sound file.
Stop/Play – This option at the bottom-left corner lets you preview all the settings you have made.

Lesson 14
Using Multiple Layers

In Flash, multiple layers are really multiple Timelines. The images contained in layers are stacked above and below other layers, but their primary purpose is to provide you with separate Timelines in which you can control animations independently. In this lesson you're going to make two circles that will move across the screen. One will appear to move faster than the other.

1. In a new file, select Oval, pick up a color and draw a circle on the left-middle of the Stage. You have to select the color right now because later you won't be able to change it.

2. Convert the circle to a symbol naming it Circle, leave the behavior set to the default Movie Clip, and click OK.

3. Now you'll name this layer Fast indicating that the circle in this layer will move fast. We are naming this layer to keep things from getting too complicated. To do so, double-click on the word Layer 1 and type Fast.

4. Position the circle at the proper place on the left side, then click and enable (F6) Frame 31, and then move the circle all the way to the right side of the Stage.

5. Select keyframe 1 and apply Motion Tween as shown in picture 4.5.

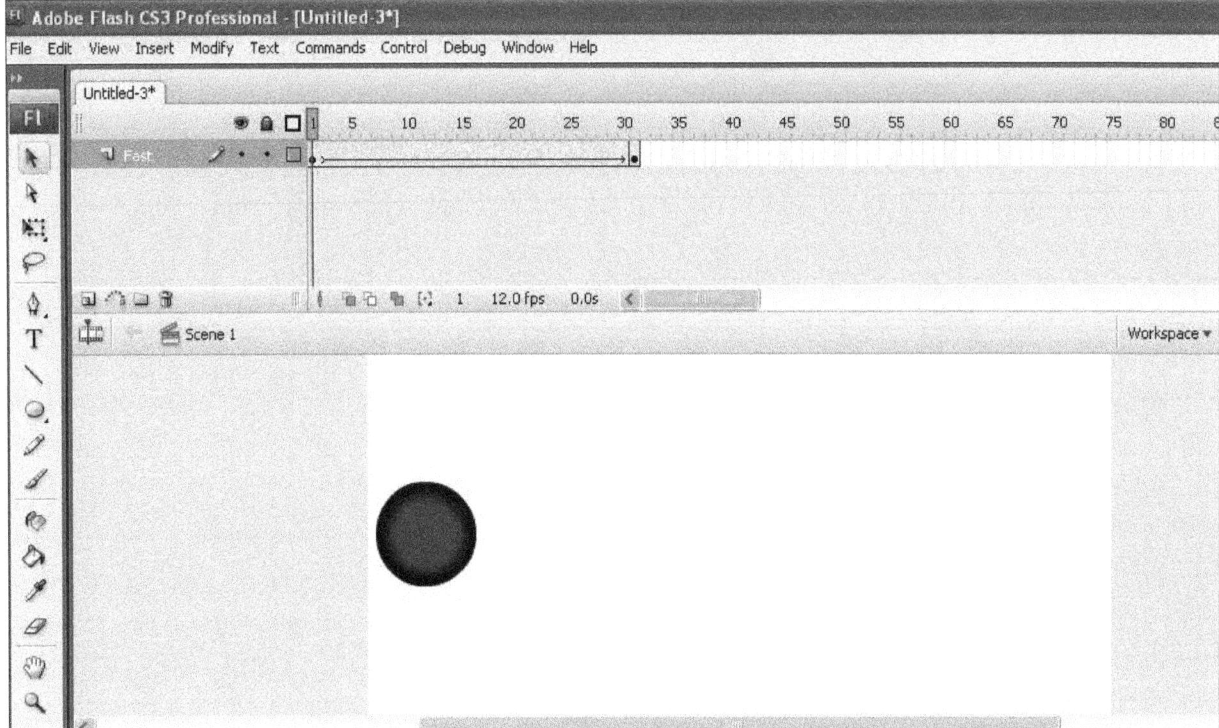

Picture 4.5

6. Create a new layer by either going to Insert> Timeline> Layer or directly right-clicking on layer and select Insert Layer. Name this new layer Slow. Now you have to be conscious of the layer in which you are editing because you can be in only one layer at a time, and the active layer is indicated by the pencil icon in the layer.

7. Next you'll copy an instance of Circle from the Fast layer and paste it in the Slow layer. To do this, select the layer Fast, click on keyframe 1 and press Ctrl + C. Then select layer Slow, click on keyframe 1 and press Ctrl + V. Position the copy of the Circle on the left but a little down so that it doesn't cover the other.

8. In the layer Slow, enable keyframe 31, and move the circle all the way to the right but a little behind the previous one. Then in Properties, select Tint from Color dropdown and you can change the color using the slider next to it as shows in picture 4.6.

9. Set the Motion Tween for the Slow layer also and test the movie.

You see two circles moving across the screen that means two things animating at once. Layers can be useful for organization and stacking purpose and they are absolutely necessary for animation effects in Flash. Save this file in normal .fla format so that you can use the same in next lesson.

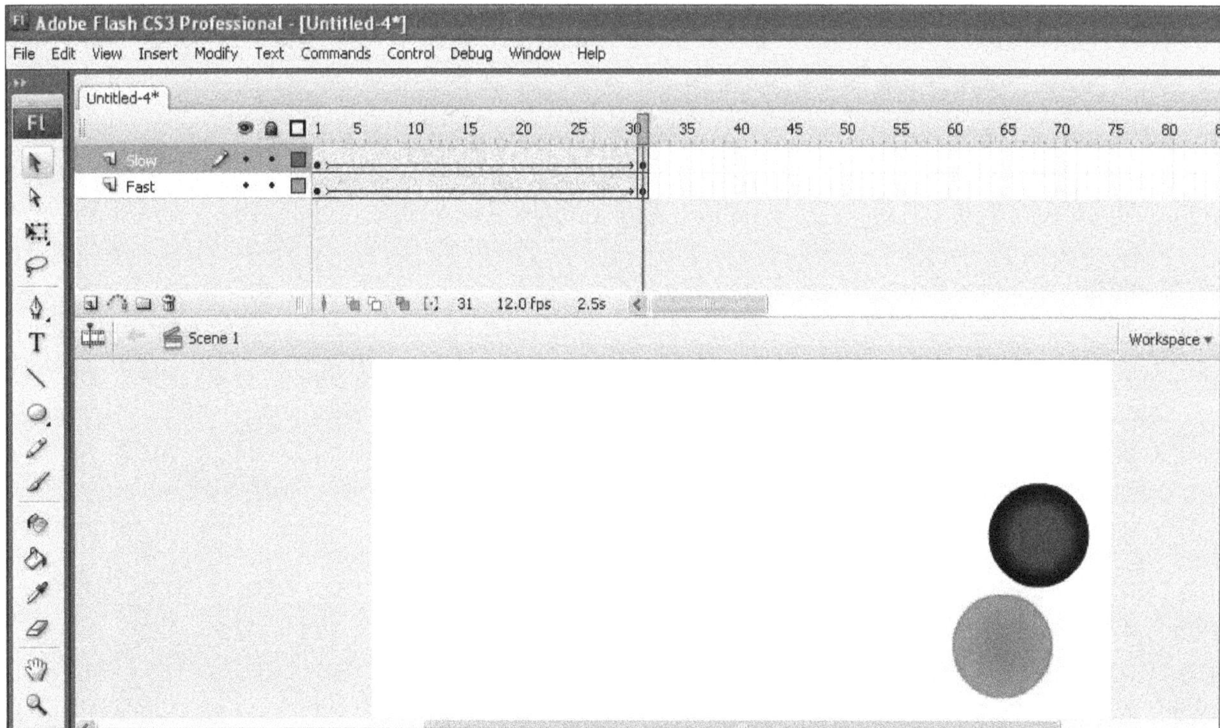

Picture 4.6

Now we'll have a look at Layer Properties by double-clicking on the small icon behind the name of the layer Fast as shown in picture 4.7.

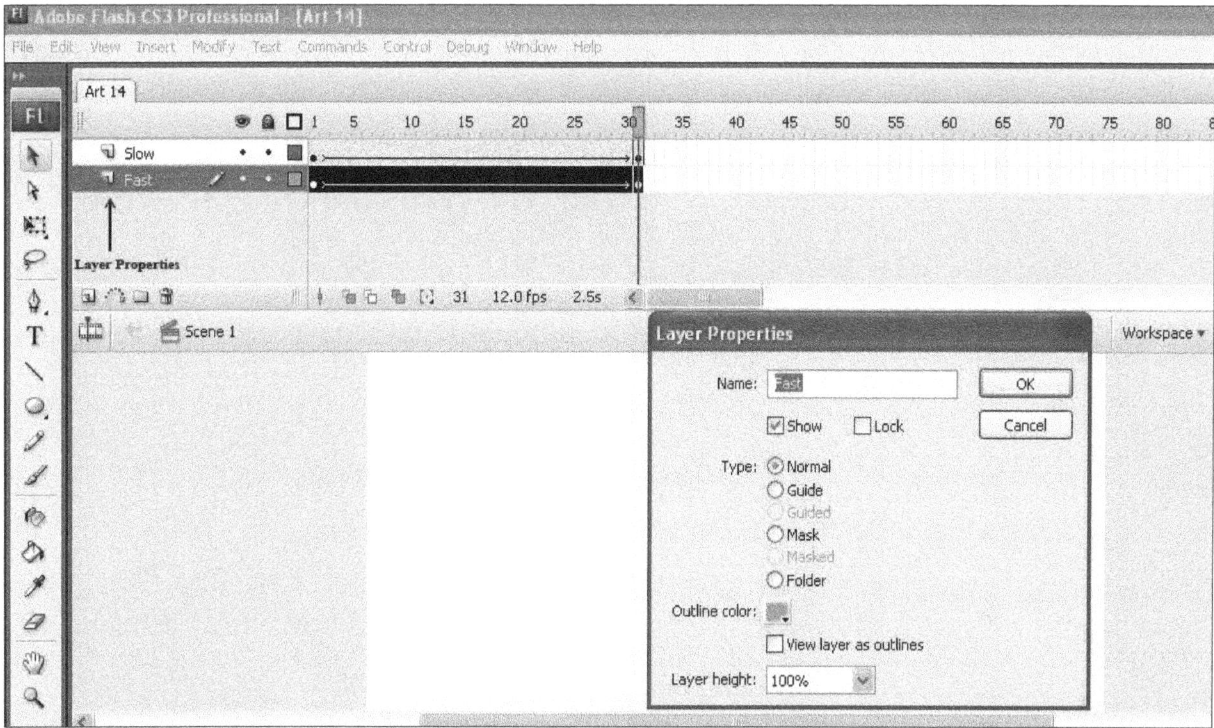

Picture 4.7

Name – This property lets you change the name of layer.
Show/Hide – It allows you to hide the content of any individual layer temporarily.
Lock/Unlock – This property lets you individually lock or unlock layers selectively or all at once.
Normal – This layer is the default type that enables the Stage to look like a plain page.
Guide – If this layer is activated, it helps you align shapes, graphics or notes to other things on stage.
Mask – It makes any shape of movie clip visible or non-visible of the layer below which is set to Masked.

Lesson 15
Visual Effects using Guide Layer

The four layer types such as Guide, Motion Guide, Mask, and Masked are very powerful in Flash. This and the following lessons are prepared especially to teach you how to use these layers for visual effects. Into a Guide Layer, you can draw lines or shapes to which other objects can snap for consistent positioning. For example, you want a title to appear in several section of a movie. If you draw a horizontal line into a Guide Layer, all the titles can be snapped to that line. But when the movie is exported, no one will see the line.

Here you're going to build a presentation that includes onscreen text and a graphic frame that provides borders. You'd like to position the text onscreen without overlapping the borders. A shape in a Guide Layer can serve to define the areas that are safe for text.

1. In a new file, select the Rectangle tool and turn of Object Drawing. Draw a filled (color-filled) box the size of the Stage. You can take the help of Info Panel in Properties also while doing this. Then select Pencil tool and set Pencil Mode option to Smooth as shown in picture 4.8.

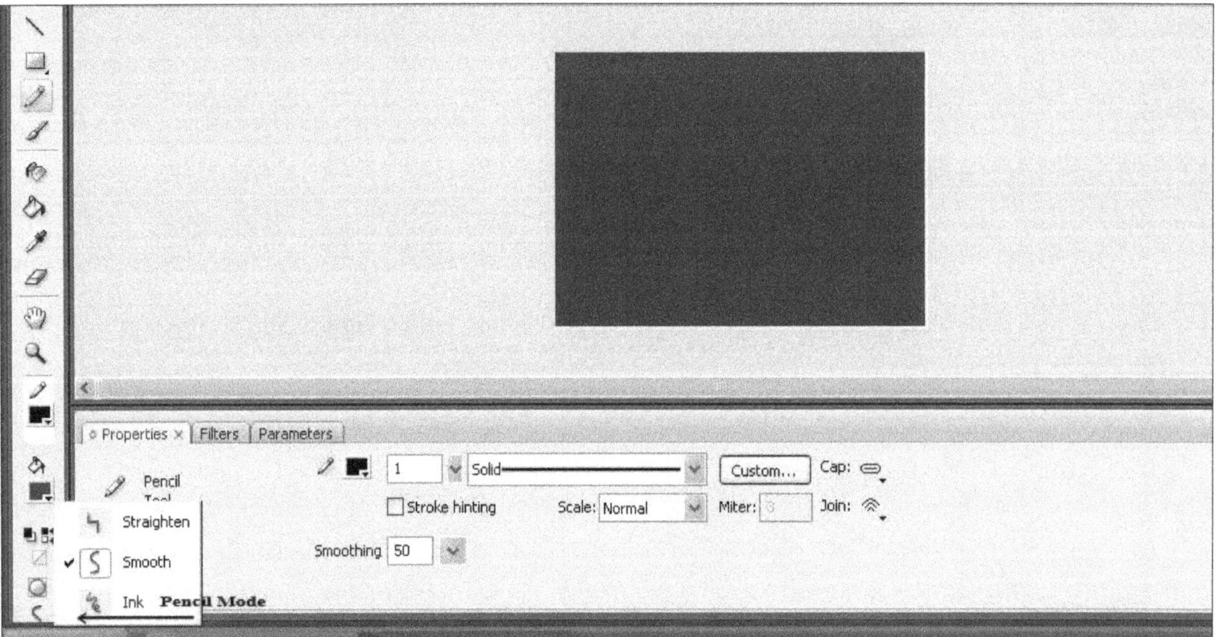

Picture 4.8

2. Using Pencil with Smooth option enabled, draw an enclosed irregular box within the box you just drew. After that, select the center shape with the Selection too and delete. Your stage will look like as shown in picture 4.9.

Picture 4.9

3. Change the name of this layer to Registration. Go to Insert> Timeline> Layer and insert a new layer which you can name Interface. On this Interface layer, a copy of Frame Shape wills tween into place late in the Timeline.

4. Now click on Frame 1 of Registration layer and you'll see that everything (Frame Shape) gets selected, so copy it by pressing Ctrl + C and click on Interface layer and enable Frame 25. And then press Ctrl + Shift + V (or go to Edit> Paste in Place). Make sure you press all these three keys, not just Ctrl + V.

5. Enable Frame 35 of Interface layer. Select Frame 25 of Interface layer and scale (enlarge) the Frame Shape much larger so that you can't actually see the borders onscreen (as in picture 5.0).

Picture 5.0

6. Set Motion Tween when Frame 25 is selected in Interface layer.

7. Click in Frame 35 of the Registration layer and press just F5 (not F6). This F5 will insert a frame (not keyframe) there which means this layer will last as long as Interface layer.

8. Click the Layer Outline button of the Registration layer (shown in picture 5.1), so only this layer will show the outline. When you scrub from beginning to the end of the movie, you'll notice that the outlined Registration layer gives a clear idea where Frame Shape will eventually appear.

9. Now we'll make Registration layer a Guide layer. So double click on Layer Properties dialog box and select Guide radio button and click Ok.

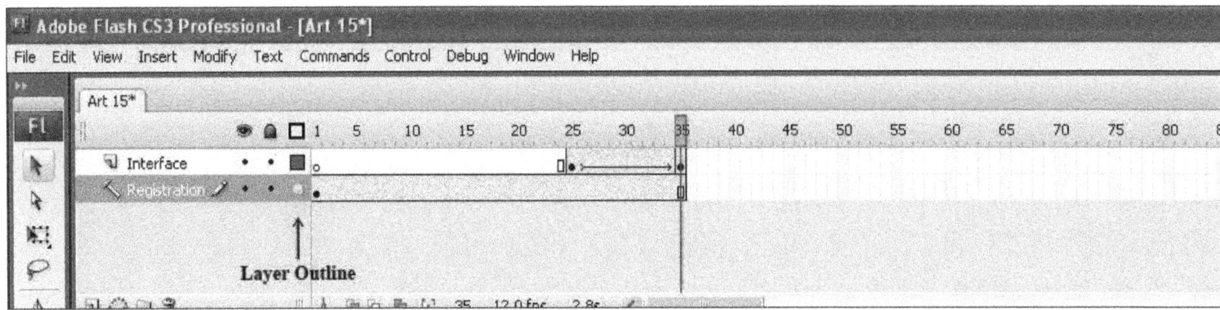

Picture 5.1

10. Insert a new layer and name this layer Text. Verify that all the layers are set to normal except Registration which should be set to Guide. Now in Frame 1 of the Text layer, create a block of the text with a large font size such as 40. Type as much text as you can but don't let it exceed the borders shown in the outline in the Registration layer (see picture 5.2). You can test the movie after typing the text.

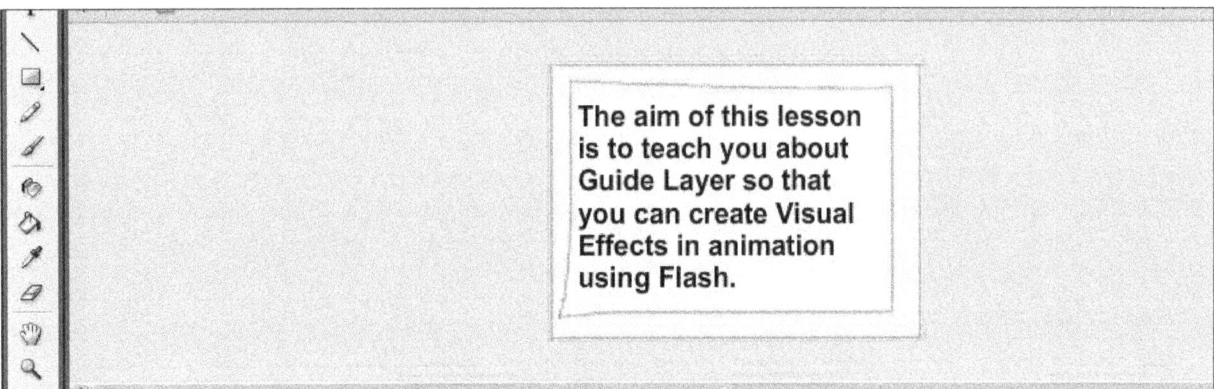

Picture 5.2

Lesson 16
Motion Guide Layers

Guide Layers are pretty useful, but Motion Guide layers are much more exciting. A Motion Guide layer is actually a regular Guide layer that happens to have an adjacent layer (below it) set to Guided. The exciting part is that a motion tween in the Guided layer will follow any path drawn in the Motion Guide layer.

In the lesson you're going to use a Motion Guide layer to produce a bouncing ball animation.

1. In a new file, draw a bouncing line using the Pencil or Pen tool (see picture 5.3). Your bouncing ball is going to follow this path. For this, you can draw straight lines also and then bend them and snap them together. It doesn't need to be perfect as it is going to be a guided and will remain invisible. Just make sure that it doesn't overlap at all.

2. Name this layer Path and change its type to Guide by going to Layer Properties dialog box.

3. Insert a new layer and name it Ball by using Layer Properties.

4. Most likely the Ball layer will appear above the Path layer. In order to make it follow the drawing in the Path layer, you must drag the Ball layer down below Path layer.

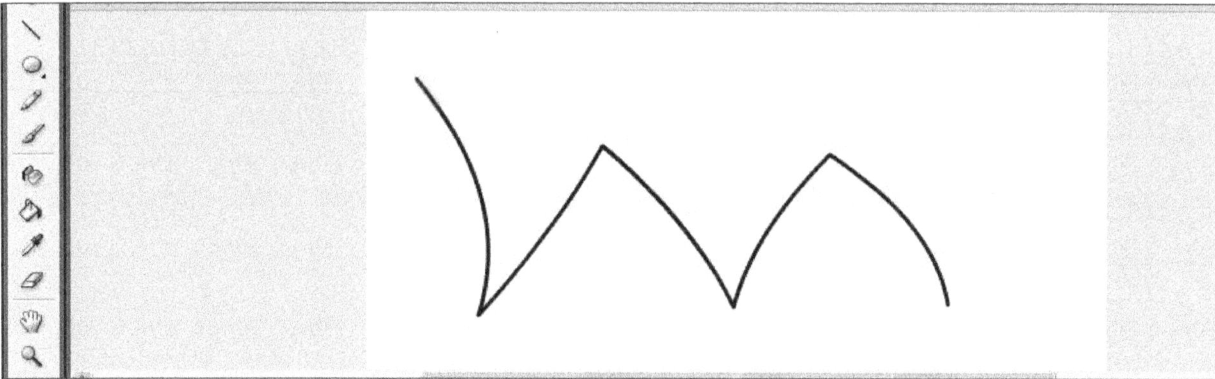

Picture 5.3

After you drag, you'll notice that now Path has a slightly different icon (the arch) with dashed line as shown in picture 5.4. In addition to that, if you go to Ball layer properties, if will find that it has already changed the Ball layer to Guided which you exactly wanted. If it is not changed, you can go to Ball layer properties and changed it to Guided. The undo command will help you go one step back if you commit any mistake.

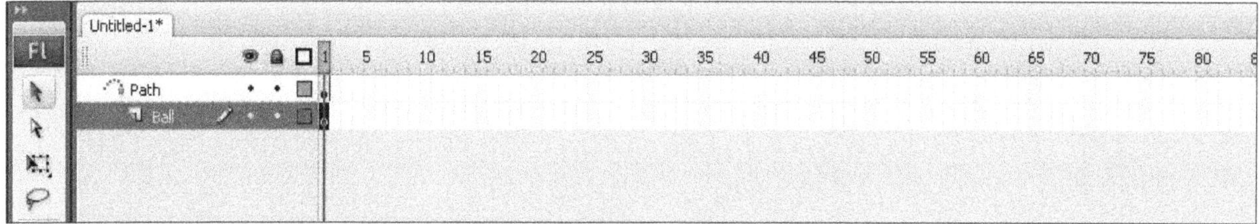

Picture 5.4

5. In Frame 1 of the Ball layer, draw a circle which should look like a ball and convert it to symbol.

6. Click and enable Frame 50 of Ball layer but you will see that Path layer doesn't last that long. In order to make Path layer go to that point, you have to insert a frame (not keyframe) by pressing just F5.

7. Select Frame 1 of the Ball layer and snap the center of the ball at the starting point of the line drawn. Go to Frame 50 of the same layer and snap the center of the ball at the ending point of the line drawn (see picture 5.5)

8. To be on the safer side, you can lock the Guide layer by clicking the dot under the padlock in the Path layer (see picture 5.5). Go back to Frame 1 of the Ball layer and create a motion tween. That's it! Test the movie now.

The ball should follow the path if the line is not overlapping. It may be possible that because of some mistake the ball is not moving the way you want. Don't quit, tray all over again. The main things are that the line should not be overlapping but snapped together, the line layer should be changed to Guide, the ball should be converted to symbol and layer should be changed to Guided, and don't forget to apply motion tween at the end.

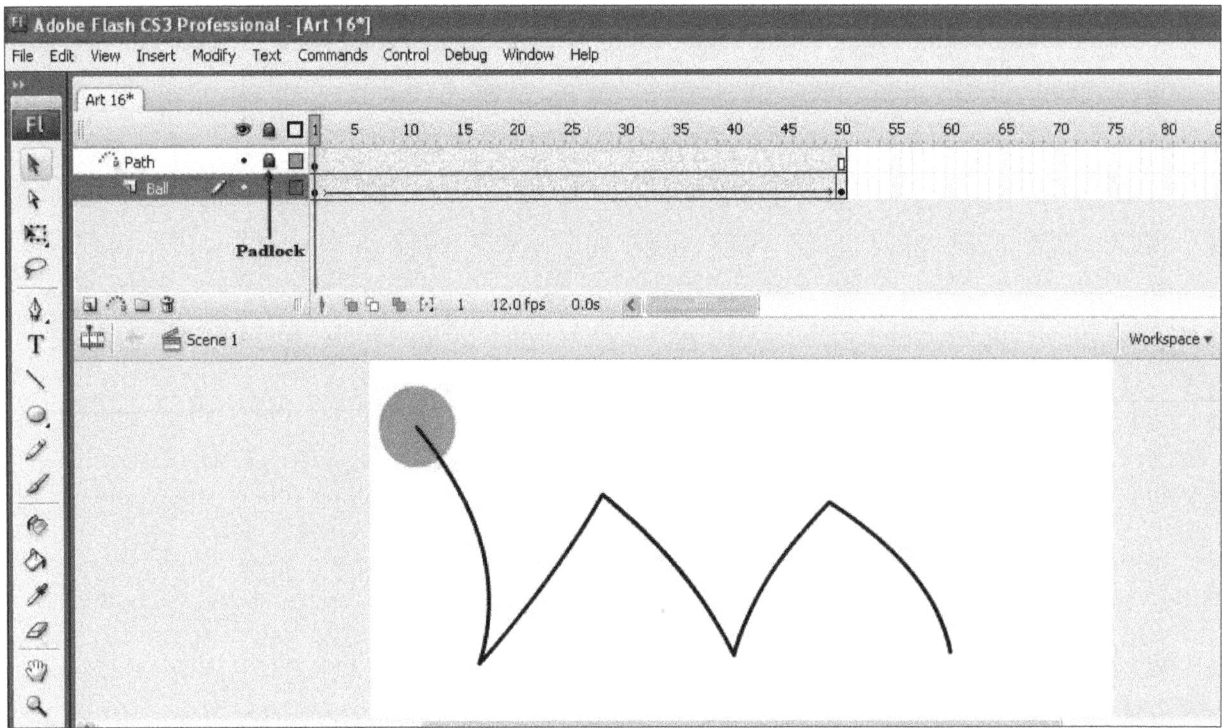

Picture 5.5

Lesson 17
Spotlight Effect

Spotlight Effect is amazing and exhilarating thing of Flash. You can create this effect in a movie clip, still image, or text image to light up the particular part of it. To say in simple words, if you have a movie or image in the background, the spotlight will keep on moving on the Stage lighting up the particular part of it. Just keep it in mind that you can see Spotlight Effect only when you test the movie or lock al the layers involved.

1. In a new file, draw a color-filled circle and covert it into a symbol naming it Spot. Let the Movie Clip option in the box remain selected as default.

2. Name this layer Spot Motion from Layer Properties.

3. Enable Frames 10, 20, 30, 40, and 50 by inserting keyframes. In Frame 10 move the spot toward right side of the Stage, and move it again for 20, 30, and 40. Frame 50 should match the Frame 1.

4. Set up motion tweening in Frames 1 to 10, 10 to 20, 20 to 30, 30 to 40 and 40 to 50. Holding Shift key down you can select all and the effect at once.

5. Go to the Layer Properties of this and change the Spot Motion layer's type to Mask. You'll notice that Page Curl icon of it changes to Mask icon.

6. Insert a new layer, name it Background, and drag it down below Spot Motion. Go to its Layer Properties and change its type to Masked.

7. In Background layer, either you can put an image, or movie clip, or image of a text. Don't rush off, just hold your horses. It is not done yet. In this layer, for this time I'm putting a picture image. You can do the same. Click File> Import> and import a JPEG file to Flash's Library.

If you don't want an image, you can create some colorful shapes also, but make sure they are ungrouped shapes and not Drawing Objects. You can also place a movie clip symbol – but only one at a time. If you want to use text, when you select Text tool, make sure under Properties on left side the text type is selected to Static text. Just to inform you that Flash has certain limitations with Spotlight Effect, so you have to bear with this. Moreover, you can change the Stage (background) color also, for that, make sure you're in Frame 1 of Background layer, click on the Stage, in Properties you see the option to change Background color.

8. When you're in Frame 1 of Background layer, go to Windows> Library and drag and drop the image on the Stage as shown in picture 5.6. Position the image on the Stage as per your choice.

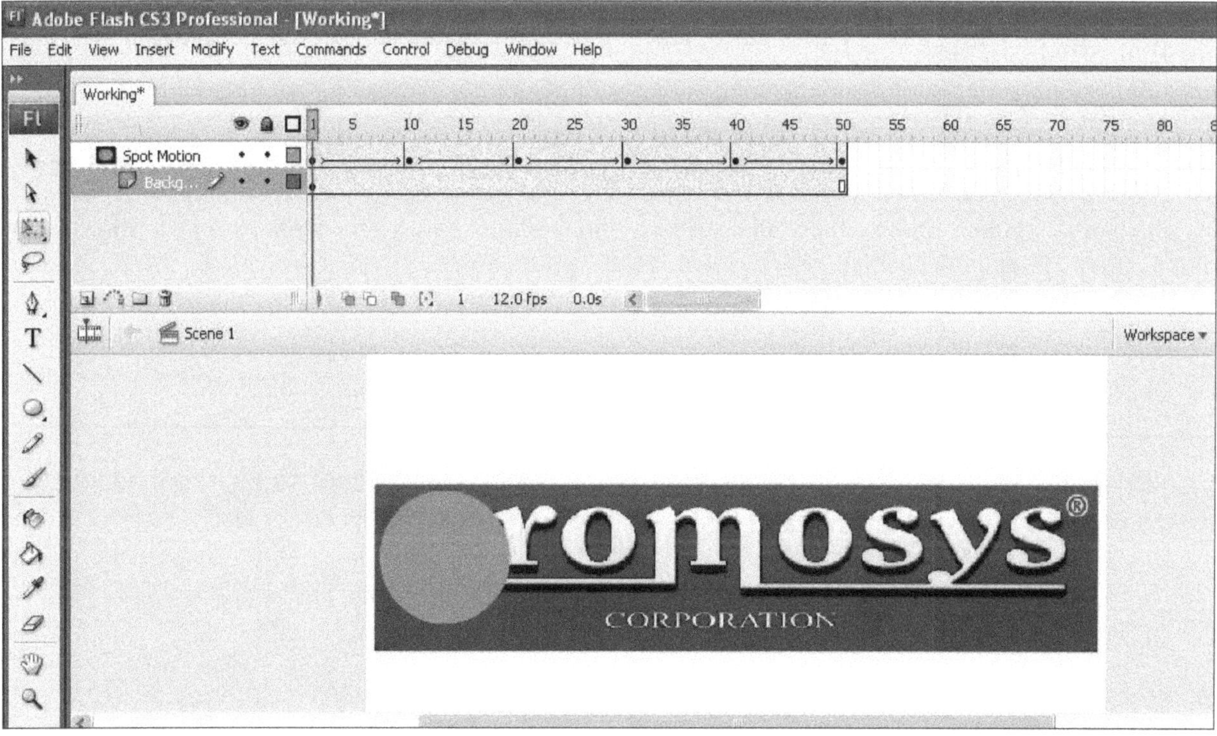

Picture 5.6

9. Click on Frame 1 of Background layer to select the image you just put on stage (or to select all the shapes you've create) and covert them to Symbol while having Movie Clip option checked. You can use the shortcut key F8 for that, and name the symbol Graphic.

10. Though pressing Ctrl + Enter you can the amazement of this animation, but I would suggest you to make it look more realistic. For that, add one more layer, name it Dim Image, and drag it down below the Background layer. If the Dim Image is automatically set to Masked, change it to Normal.

11. Copy the instance of Background layer and do Paste in Place by pressing Ctrl + Shift + V (not just Ctrl + V) in the Frame 1 of Dim Image layer.

12. Select Frame 1 in Dim Image, go to Properties, select Brightness in the dropdown of Color and set it to +40. Lock all the layers if you want, and then press Ctrl + Enter to get wowed!

A step ahead with Spotlight Effect
It gives marvelous effect to your animation. Suppose you're building an animation of someone insisting inside a train, and you want the effect of mountain of clouds passing by the window. You can do it in a minute or two. Here is what you need for this. Draw a filled rectangle which looks like a window. Convert it to a symbol and move at a three different place in three different keyframes. Set Motion Tween to all of them. From Layer Properties, change its type to Mask. Insert layer 2, drag it down below layer 1 and set it to Masked type. Import and drag a good picture on the Stage. Convert it to symbol. You can change the background (stage) color if you want. Insert frame by pressing F5 in layer 2 at the same point where Layer 1 end. That's it! Test the movie and get thrilled.

Lesson 18
Creating Blend Effect

Blend mode feature gives you a powerful and more complex way to perform masking. If you've worked on Photoshop, you should know what blend is. Blends define how overlapping instances composite each other in visual effects. With Alpha, Invert, Darken options of it, you can change your image look like a negative or completely dark on the Stage. Suppose you want to show a new car in your animation but first you want a light effect, then a dark view of the car getting brighter, and then you want the car to be shown in full shine. You can do all this using Blend here.

1. In a new file, import a good picture of car and drag it to the stage. Convert it to symbol and name it Car.

2. Insert layer 2 and let it remain by default above layer 1 (don't drag it down). Copy the symbol from layer 1 and do Paste in Place using Ctrl + Shift + V in Layer 2.

3. Draw a filled rectangle over the picture of car having Object Drawing enabled. Select the rectangle; convert it to symbol naming it Light.

4. Having Light symbol selected, go to Properties and select Multiply from Blend option (see picture 5.7). For your knowledge, you can see the effects of some other options.

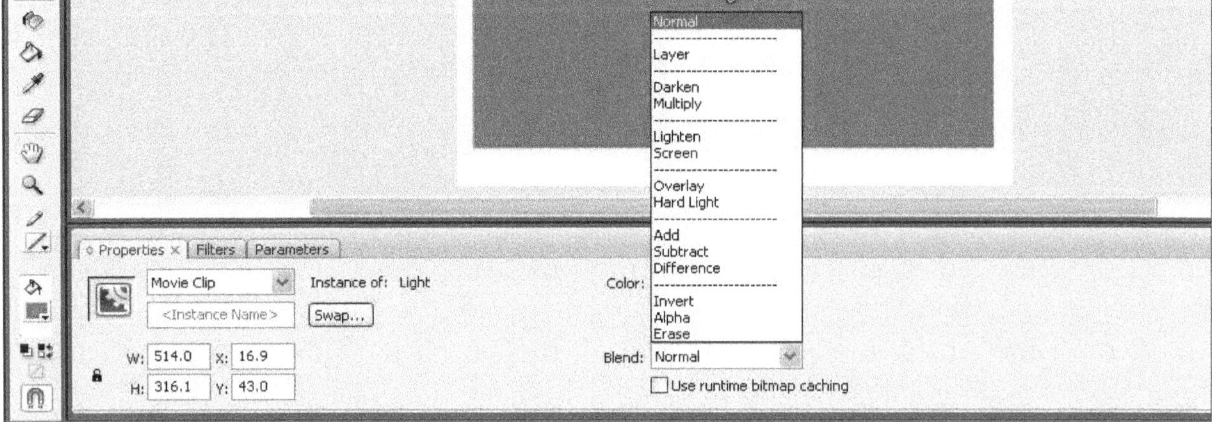

Picture 5.7

5. Now enable keyframe 20 in layer 2, select only Light symbol on Stage and delete it. Select the Car symbol on Stage which is left behind, go to Properties, and select Brightness from Color dropdown. You can set the brightness to -70 (minus).

6. Select Frame 1 in layer 2, with Selection Tool, draw a selection line around the entire instance of Stage so that the Light symbol along with car symbol behind can be selected together.

7. Convert the selection to symbol naming it Start, and set Motion Tween between Frame 1 and 20 in layer 2 which is still above layer 1 (don't drag it down).

8. Enable keyframe 30 in layer two and drag and drop the Car symbol on the Stage matching in place with Start symbol.

9. Enable keyframe 35 also to give a pause and test a movie pressing Ctrl + Enter. I am sure you'll like this animation. To create this kind of Blend Effect, now you can find out some other ways also doing your own exploration.

Like this, you can create some more terrific animations on your own. To get help for one more, draw a medium size filled rectangle with blue outline. Go to Color section on right hand side panel and select Radial (or Linear) from Type dropdown. Making changes in RGB and Alpha settings and clicking back on the rectangle on Stage will help you understand color settings. Once you're done with that, you have to convert it to symbol. Enable keyframe 15 and select Overlay under Blend option. You can make some changes by selecting Brightness from Color option. This is going to be the Drop Shadow of the instance. Move the blended Drop Shadow down by an inch and set Motion Tween at keyframe 1. That's it.

Using Filters
Bring a picture on the Stage and convert it to symbol. Enable keyframe 20 and set blend effect to Hard light and under Color, Alpha to 30%. Select keyframe 1 and click on the picture, and then go to Filters tab in Properties. Click on Add Filters + sign button and select Glow. Make changes in settings and play the animation.

Lesson 19
Nesting Animation with a Rotating Wheel

You'll be blown away after you see what nesting animation can do. In this lesson, inside a Movie Clip symbol you create an animation, and then animate an instance of that clip. Keeping one master version of a drawing in Library, you can create and use as many instances of it as you like using nesting of Flash, with no significant impact on file size.

In this lesson you'll nest a clip of a wheel inside a clip that will become an animating wheel that you can use anywhere you want:

1. Draw a circle with a few lines crossing it as shown in picture 5.8. Don't think of making it perfect but let it happen as it happens. Select the entire shape and convert it to symbol naming it Wheel. As behavior type is set to Movie Clip by default, so you're going to make a Movie Clip of the wheel spinning next.

Picture 5.8

2. Select the Wheel symbol on the Stage and again convert it to symbol naming it Rotating Wheel. Don't change anything in its behavior type. The reason why converted it again is that in step 1 you put a shape in the Library, and in this step you took an instance of Wheel and put it in the Rotating Wheel symbol. It is going to be amazing, just hold your horses.

3. You have done a nesting now. To understand what nesting is, you have to pay a little bit of attention. Right now you're on the Stage of Scene 1 as it is clearly written in your edit bar which is just below the Timeline. And you have Rotating Wheel symbol on stage because the moment you create a new symbol, it leaves a copy on Stage also. In order to verify it, if you select the symbol, the Properties panel will say: Instance of: Rotating Wheel.

4. Now double-click on Rotating Wheel symbol to go into its nesting. The moment you do, the edit bar changes to Rotating Wheel stage and you get into the master version of Rotating Wheel. This means the Rotating Wheel contains an instance of Wheel.

5. While inside Rotating Wheel, we'll do a simple motion tween of the Wheel instance. To do this, enable keyframe 20, go back to Frame 1 and select Tween Motion and Rotate CW 1 time. Test the movie and you'll be really blown away. The wheel is rotating now.

6. Now to come out of nesting, click on Scene 1 of edit bar just below the Timeline. This is the stage of Scene 1, not of Rotating Wheel.

7. Drag and drop the instance of one more Rotating Wheel from Library and position them side-by-side as shown in picture 5.9.

8. Use the Brush tool to draw the car body as shown in the same picture 5.9. Select everything and convert it to symbol called Car leaving its behavior to Movie Clip.

9. Enable keyframe 30 by pressing F6 in the Timeline (this is the main Timeline of Scene 1), and move the instance of car toward right on the Stage. Select Frame 1 and apply Motion Tween. Press Ctrl + Enter and you'll jump off the chair as you'll see the car move.

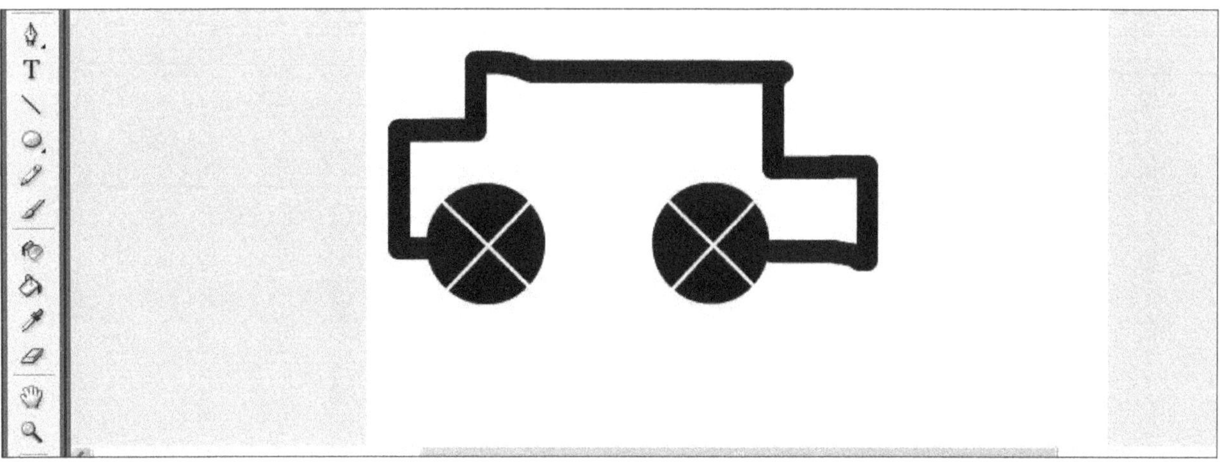

Picture 5.9

Just to rephrase what you did in nesting is that you made a Wheel symbol, and you made a Rotating Wheel symbol that contained Wheel because you needed a symbol <u>inside</u> Rotating Wheel to do a motion tween. Then you used two instances of Rotating Wheel in the creation of the Car symbol.

Lesson 20
Creating Special Effects

You have already learnt about creating and modifying gradients. In this lesson you're going to use the Color panel to select the bitmap image and use the Gradient Transform tool to modify it. By the way a bitmap graphic is one for which the computer must store information about every single pixel.

1. In a new file, open the Color panel by clicking on the Color tab at the top right and make sure the Fill Color swatch is selected (if not, you can click on it). From the Type dropdown, select Bitmap as shown in picture 6.0.

Picture 6.0

2. Select any raster (.jpg, .gif, .bmp) graphic of medium size which has the dimension of near about 500x400. If you have a big graphic, you know you can reduce the size in Photoshop by selecting Image Size option. Import the graphic to Library.

3. Select the Rectangle tool and set the stroke to "No Stroke" by clicking on the diagonal red line (see picture 6.1).

Picture 6.1

4. Draw a square on stage and you'll see that it contains your imported graphic. Pick up the Gradient Transform tool which you can access when you click and hold the Free Transform tool button in Tools panel.

5. With the Gradient Transform tool, click the fill of your square and modify the size and location of the bitmap fill. If you import a large graphic, you have to zoom out in order to see all the handles to modify the fill. Give it a proper size and location as shown in the picture 6.1, so that it occupies most of the space of the Stage.

6. Now you'll apply Mirror Hall effect on it that will drive you crazy. For that, enable keyframe 5 by pressing f6 in Timeline. Use the Selection tool to select the square on stage and open the Transform panel which is below Color panel. Type 80 into both the width and height fields, and then click ONCE on the "Copy and apply transform" button near the bottom right of the Transform panel. It will show one Mirror Hall.

7. Enable keyframe 10, enter 80 into both the width and height fields of Transform panel again and click on the "Copy and apply transform" button one more time. Like this, keep adding keyframes till Frame 20 clicking once on the same Copy and apply transform button. At keyframe 20, the result should look like picture 6.2.

Picture 6.2

8. Select all the keyframes from 1, 5, 10, 15, and 20 by holding Shift, and apply Shape Tween effect (not Motion Tween for heaven's sake, because they are not converted to symbols). Test the movie now. Tell me; was I wrong when I said it would drive you crazy?

Lesson 21
Animating a Bock of Text

Here you're going to animate each character of the text independently, and for that, you need to break apart the block of the text, and then make symbols out of each character for applying gradient plus Motion Tween effects.

1. In a new file, select the Text tool and pick a very large font size like '60', and then click on the Stage.

2. Type the word CLICK. Take the Selection tool and single click the entire block of text. Position the text at the bottom because the animation will end at this place. Choose Modify> Break Apart. Each letter is a separate block of text now.

3. With all the letters selected, choose Modify> Timeline> Distribute to Layers. All the five letters occupied their own separate layers. Select the Layer 1 (master layer), which has nothing in it now, and delete it by pressing delete key.

4. As we want to animate (motion tween) these letters, so they all need to be converted to Movie Clip symbol. For that, click once on first letter C and covert it to symbol by pressing F8, and name it C as well. Do the same for all the other letters naming them appropriately. After you're done with that, you can apply gradient color effect or leave it as it is for now.

5. Do not make any changes in the place arrangement of the letter instances. Now click once at Frame 50 of each layer and insert only a frame (F5). Then in the first C layer, enable keyframe 10 using F6, in the L layer enable keyframe 15, in the layer I enable keyframe 20, in the second C layer at 25, and in the K layer at 30.

6. Return to Frame 1 by clicking above the 1 in the Timeline. Click on the first letter C on stage, hold Shift key and drag the letter up so the letter appears above the stage. Do the same for the other letters. Finally, click the keyframe 1 in first C layer and set Motion tween. Do the same for the first keyframe in the other layers. After all done, you can test the movie to view the animation.

Lesson 22
Converting Text to a Shape for Special Effects

This lesson is going to teach you how and why will you turn text into a shape (not symbol). Once the text is changed to a shape, you can distort the text in any manner and add a stroke (color style) of your choice, or fill a gradient or bitmap. Using Selection or Sub-selection tool, you can stretch and reshape the text. The only minus point is that you can not edit the shape as text. The following steps let you understand all these options.

1. In a new file, select the Text tool and pick up a very bold font – possibly 'Impact'. Type a word of medium size in the upper middle part of stage. Take Selection tool and click once on the entire block of text you typed. Go to Modify> Break Apart. Again, without clicking anywhere (otherwise the text would get deselected), Modify> Break Apart. Now all the letters are shapes.

2. Use the Selection tool to stretch and bend the characters and reshape them anyway you want. But don't go wild. See the picture 6.3 for help which shows the result of reshaping the C character.

Picture 6.3

3. Select all the shapes by dragging over it using Selection tool, and go to Modify> Group. This will make the shape for creating the shadow. Copy the group and paste it. Position the duplicate out of the way of the original. With the duplicate selected choose Modify> Transform, Flip Vertical. Then select Modify> Ungroup. See picture 6.4 for help.

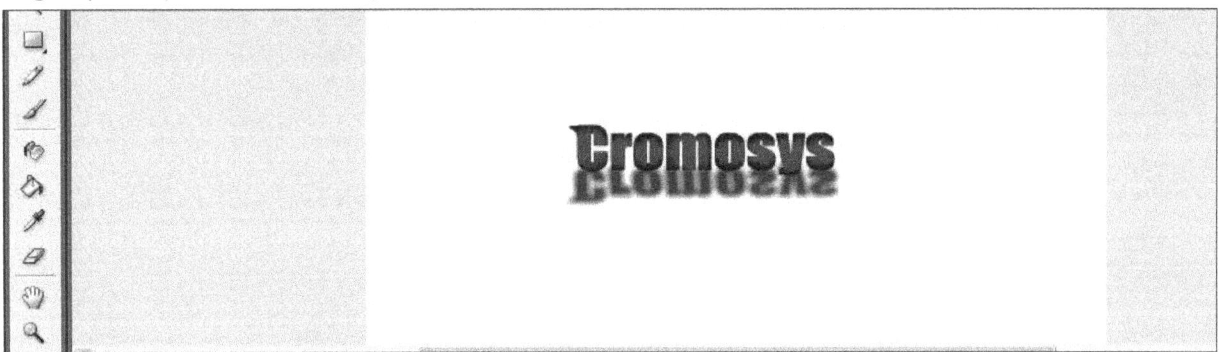

Picture 6.4

4. Use Free Transform tool to select all the shadow characters. Go to Modify> Shape> Distort, then hold the shift and drag the bottom-right corner out to make the shadow bigger if you want. You can apply lighter color on it. With all the shadow selected choose Modify> Convert to Symbol using Movie Clip.

5. Select the shadow clip and use Filters panel to apply a Blur effect. Go to Properties and change the alpha to something like 30%.

6. Now you can change the fill color on primary letters. For that, double-click to enter the primary letters' group. Select any color style from Color panel you want. In the picture 6.4 I have selected radial gradient.

7. Now we'll start animation. Go up to the main Timeline and select the main letters. Cut them by pressing Ctrl + X, insert a new layer and do Paste in Place by pressing (Ctrl + Shift + V) in this new layer.

8. Select the letters again and choose Modify> Break Apart. Finally, enable keyframe 20 and make the set of letters bigger on stage. Go to Frame 1 and set a Shape tween.

9. Select shadow (first) layer and enable keyframe 20. Use the Free Transform tool and make the shadow big enough to match the primary letters. See picture 6.5 for help. Finally, return to Frame 1 of the shadow's layer and set Motion tween. Test the movie now. You are welcome the make any change in color, shape, and design at any time.

Picture 6.5

Lesson 23
Adding a Shadow to Show Depth and Distance

In this lesson you are going to use Drop Shadow filter for depth and motion. Adding a subtle shadow can go a long way toward adding depth to your animations. Here is a great task that proves that. For any animation, if you want the original screen size (not zoom) to be bigger, the moment you open Flash, you can change the size from Properties panel from default 550x400 to any size you want.

1. In a new file, draw a circle of any color near the top-middle of the stage, select it and convert to a Movie Clip symbol.

2. Enable Frame 10 and 20 by inserting keyframes. Now that Frames 1 and 20 are the same, go to Frame 10 and hold Shift while you drag the instance of the circle down almost to the bottom of the stage.

3. Select Frames 1 and 10 holding Shift key and set Motion tween. Select the circle instance and copy it pressing Ctrl + C (you'll use it in next step). Name the sole layer Circle and then lock the layer. Insert a new layer and name it Shadow. You must drag the Shadow layer down below Circle layer.

4. In the Shadow layer at Frame 1, do Paste in Place. The instance you just copied will appear there. Use the Free Transform tool to give it the size you want. Just keep it in mind that it is going to be the shadow of the primary circle. Select the instance with Selection tool, and in Properties set Blend to Invert, and Color to Alpha 57%. Keep the shadow selected and use Filters to set Blur with both X and Y direction to 20. Here you may use your own skills to make it more realistic. You are free to use any tool you want. The next picture 6.6 may help you a little for this.

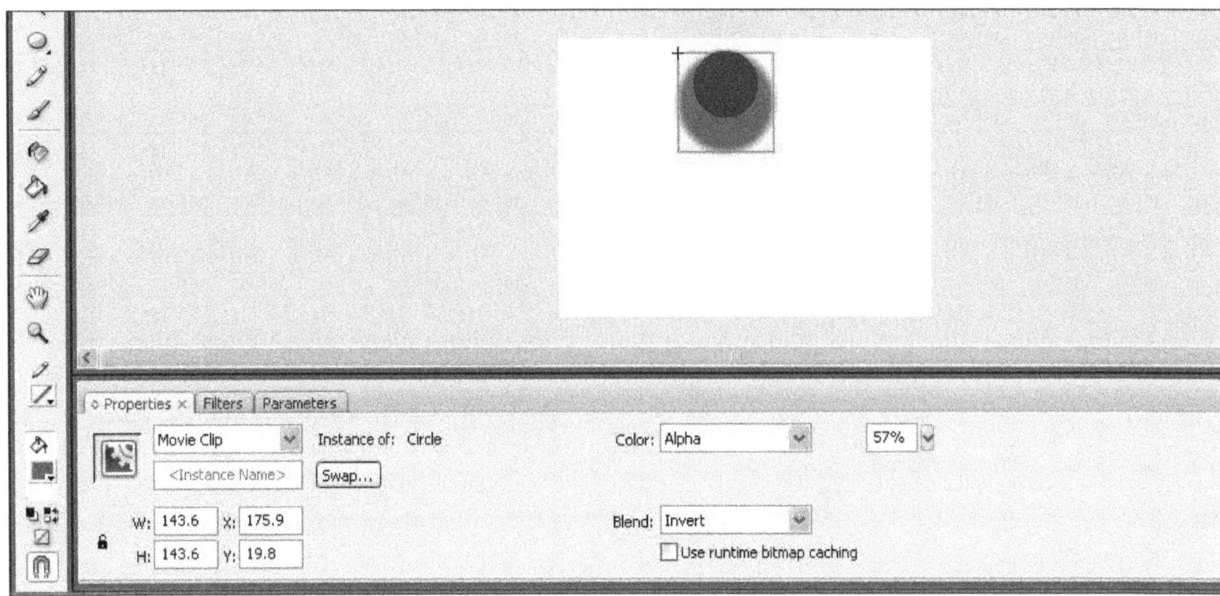

Picture 6.6

5. Enable Frame 10 and 20 in Shadow layer by inserting keyframes. Click Frame 10, select the shadow and holding Shift key drag it down so that it comes below the primary circle when it hits the bottom. Now at frame 10 of Shadow layer you can increase the Blur size if you want. Here you're exposed to the artistic world, and you can use your own skill as much you want. The next picture 6.7 is just a help for you.

Picture 6.7

6. When all set, click Frames 1 and 10 and set Motion tween. Test the movie now. I think it is okay but you can use your talent to make it better.

Lesson 24
Creating a Magnifier Effect with Masking

Here you're going to add realism to your masking effect and that will result in masking the text on the screen.

1. Draw a circle in a new file, convert it to a Movie Clip symbol, and name it Circle. Name the sole layer Circle.

2. Insert a new layer and name this layer Big Text. Select the Text tool and set the font about as tall as your circle was drawn, and set the text type to Static from Properties. Click on Stage and type one long word. Use the Selection tool to move the text so the circle covers the first letter in our word; then convert the block of text into a Movie Clip symbol named MyText. Drag the Big Text layer down below the Circle layer. Set the Circle layer to Mask, and Big Text layer to Masked.

3. Because we want the mask to magnify the text, we need a small version of the text underneath everything else. Insert a new layer and name this layer Small Text. Drag this layer below the other tow layers. If the Small Text layer gets automatically set to Masked, then set it back to Normal. Click on My Text layer and copy the instance of it from stage. Go to Small Text layer and do Paste in Place. Select the Free Transform tool, hold Shift, and resize MyText instance (in the Small Text layer) so it's about 80% of the original size.

4. Now the issue is that while the large text is revealed by the mask, you can see through to the small text underneath. You only want to see through where the mask isn't. This is really simple to fix: the text needs an opaque background. For that, open the Library and double-click on MyText symbol (it will show the Edit bar changed). Select the Rectangle tool; choose white color and "no stroke". Then draw a rectangle at least as big as the block of text. Select the drawn rectangle and go to Modify> Arrange> Send to Back. Go back to your main Timeline by clicking on Scene 1 tab in Edit bar. See the picture 6.8 for Timeline help.

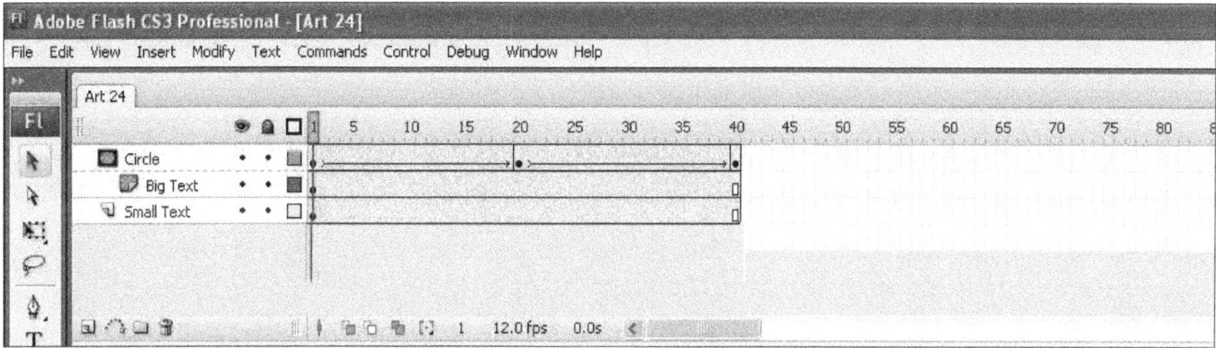

Picture 6.8

5. At this point we can tween the Circle. For each layer click the cell in Frame 40 and insert a frame (F5). For the Circle layer add a keyframe at Frame 20 and another at 40. Go back to Frame 20 and move the circle so that it covers the rightmost letter in your MyText instance. Set Motion tween for Frames 1 and 15 in the Circle layer and test the movie. See the picture 6.9 for help.

6. To apply realism now, double-click on circle icon in Library. Select the circle, open the Color panel and select radial gradient. With the Circle's fill still selected, edit the gradient so the while is 0% alpha. Don't test the movie because you'll see no change at this time as the mast is either on or off.

7. Go back to main Timeline by clicking Scene 1 on Edit bar of stage, and insert another layer named Front. Drag this Front layer above all the layers and make sure its properties is set to Normal. Now click once on Circle layer's name and it will select all the frames of the layer automatically by blackening the entire line. Then right click on any frame in the Circle layer and select Copy Frames.

8. Right click into Frame 1 of Front layer and select Paste Frames. The Front layer will get extended longer than all the other layers. In that case, remove the excess frames by holding Ctrl and dragging the end frame all the way to the left. Finally your Timeline along with the Stage should look as shown in picture 6.9. You can test the movie now.

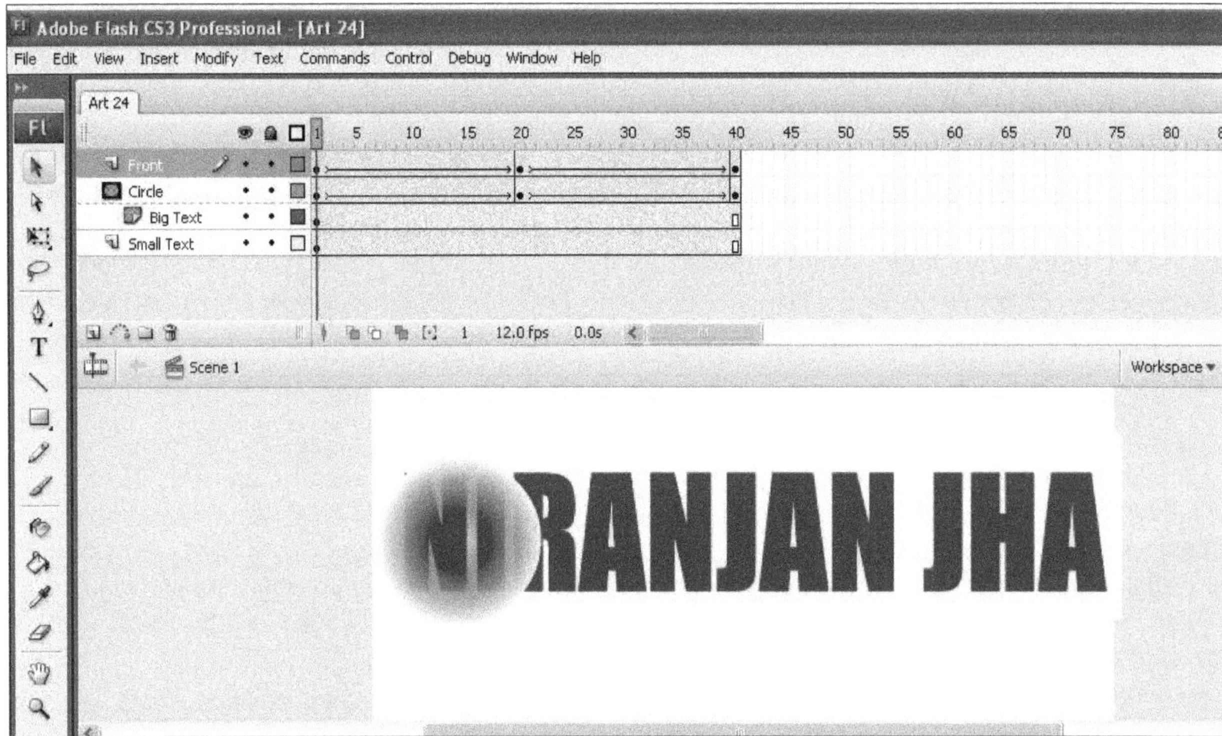

Picture 6.9

Lesson 25
Create a Hand-drawn Making Transition

You're going to create an animation that will look like someone is changing the image by painting one line at a time.

1. Import a new image file to Library and drag it to the Stage. Place it at 0x 0y by entering numeric zero in Properties. Name this layer Start and press F5 at Frame 60.

2. Insert second layer above Start and name it Transition. This layer should automatically last 60 frames, if not, insert frame at 60. Select the Brush tool, make sure Object Drawing is turned off, and paint one little blob in the top left corner of the image (see picture 7.0). Your Brush size should be nice and large.

3. Enable keyframe 5 by pressing F6 and paint a little more joining it with previous blob. Then enable keyframe 10 and paint a little more again in the continuation of covering the image. Like this, keep adding keyframes after every 5 frames and paint a little further so that by keyframe 55 the entire image is painted. You can add some more keyframes if needed but make sure at the end entire image is painted. See picture 7.1 for help.

4. When you're done with painting, set Transition layer to Mask and Stat layer to Masked. You can test the movie but I don't think you'll like it at this moment.

Picture 7.0

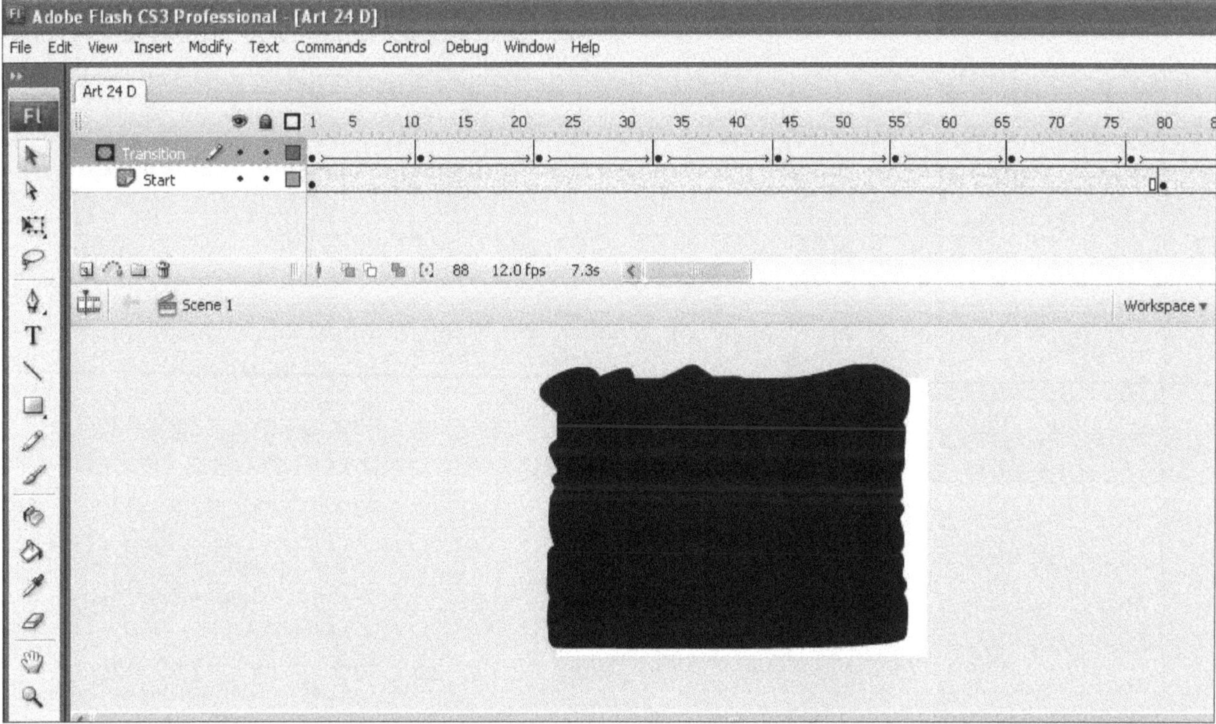

Picture 7.1

5. Select all the keyframes starting from 1 to 50 by holding Shift key down (no need to select 55) and apply Shape tween effect. As you know it won't take Motion tween because the blobs drawn are not converted to symbol. Now test the movie pressing Ctlr + Enter.

The Special Effects that you learnt in most of t these lessons, they can be applied on text, image, logo or anything else for that matter. The aim of this book is to show you the way so that you can explore on your own. Flash doesn't end here nor does Special Effects. Now it's your turn to imagine things and create the more complex designs. With the next lesson, you're going to start Flash's programming language called ActionScript. Don't' lose your interest, just continue learning.

ActionScript

Flash's programming language that is called ActionScript, like any other coding it lets you write instructions that your movie will follow. Before starting this lesson, I ought to say that ActionScript is so big that this entire book is too small to cover it fully. And for those, who're amateur and not serious in learning Flash, ActionScript would be challenging to them. Though I have included only easy and simple coding in this book to just let you understand the basic platform of it, yet not being attentive to it will lead you nowhere. And I believe once you're thorough with the basic of ActionScript, later if needed, you can enhance your knowledge with the help of any other book especially written for Flash's programming.

Coding or scripting is like writing instructions to "play" or "stop" or do something specific in Flash. All the script is typed in Actions panel. Go to Windows> Actions (F9) and take a quick look at features on your Flash's screen and read their names from picture 7.2. All the features are numbered for your convenience. Their functions are explained in the next page of the book.

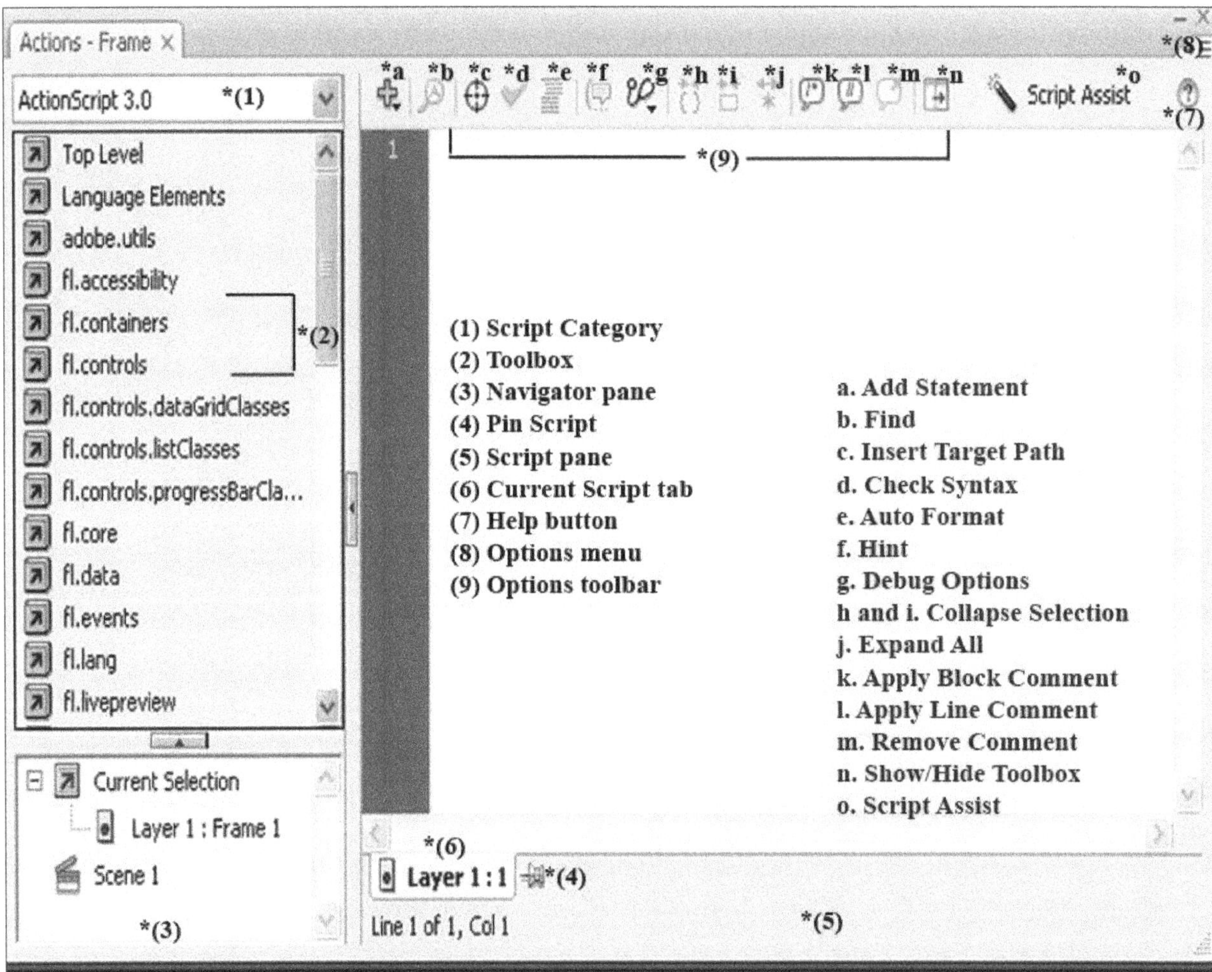

Picture 7.2

1. Script Category – simply narrows the actions listed in the toolbox to ActionScript 3.0. ActionScript 1.0 and 2.0 are used for mobile devices.
2. Toolbox – provides access to all installed actions. It is organized like folders.

3. Navigator pane – shows all the scripts in your movie.

4. Pin Script – adds a tab for a particular script so that you don't have to first select the object or layer into which you want to add a script.

5. Script pane – shows your actions for execution.

6. Current Script tab – indicates which script is currently being edited.

7. Help button – provides online help with any selected piece of ActionScript.

8. Options menu – contains additional settings such as script font.

9. Options toolbar – It includes several buttons which are explained in the next section of the lesson.

The buttons of the Options toolbar:

a. The button Add Statement or generally called "plus button" – It pops up a menu that provided the same script elements found in the Toolbox. The menu also shows the key combination for each script.

b. Find – It lets you search scripts as you do in word-processing program.

c. Insert Target Path – This button helps you address specific objects, such as particular clips on which you can apply script.

d. Check Syntax – This button checks that your ActionScript has no syntax errors and displays details in the Output panel.

e. Auto Format – It cleans up your code by adding indentation where appropriate. This makes it much easier to read.

f. Hint – It re-triggers the code-completion helper that appears as a ToolTip to help you complete ActionScript when Flash knows what you're abou to type.

g. Debug Options – This button lets you add and remove breakpoints where you purposefully make Flash pause on a specified line of code so that you can investigate how it's playing, or, not playing the way you expected.

h and i. Collapse Selection (Collapse Between Braces and Collapse Selection) – These options trigger "code folding" on parts of your script. When your script gets very long, collapsing code lets you hide the parts on which you're finished working.

j. Expand All – This lets you quickly expand any code previously collapsed.

k. Apply Block Comment – It helps you write notes to yourself for a particular coding.

l. Apply Line Comment – Whereas block comments can include multiple lines, a single line comment can be written using this option.

m. Remove Comment – This is just a quick way to remove any selected comments.

n. Show/Hide Toolbox – This button is much easier to open and close the Toolbox while writing scripts.

o. Script Assist – When this button is clicked you no longer type free-style into the script pane, but rather you make selections from options that will appear above the script pane. It also ensures your scripts are free of syntax errors.

ActionScript is just an instruction that Flash follow line after line. Just to remind you that Flash has no mercy for invalid syntax. When you test the movie you'll see errors appear in the Output panel until you resolve the errors.

Lesson 26
Applying a Loop Action

In this lesson you're going to use ActionScript to make the last few frames of an animation loop. Please follow these steps carefully without any mistake.

1. Open Flash program as usual selecting (ActionScript 3.0), and type the word **Start**. Make sure the text type is Static. Select the block and convert it to a Movie Clip symbol naming it **Start Text**.

2. Position the movie clip instance in the center of the Stage, and insert keyframes at Frame 20 and another at Frame 30.

3. Select Frame 1 and move the Start Text all the way off the Stage to the left. Select Frames 1 and 20 and apply Motion Tween. In Frame 20, make the tween rotate one time clockwise (CW) on its way from Frame 20 to Frame 30. Name this layer **Animation**. If you test the movie at this time, the whole movie loops over and over. Now you're going to make the rotation part (from Frame 20 to Frame 30) loop forever without affecting the first part (from Frame 1 to Frame 20).

4. Though ActionScript can be added in the same layer where animation is, but for convenience you can add a new layer naming it **Actions**. Insert keyframe at Frame 30 of Actions layer.

5. Make sure Fame 30 in Actions layer is still selected, then press F9 to open Actions panel. The Current Script tab will also confirm your current-frame location as it reads "Actions:30" and has the keyframe icon as shown in picture 7.3. That means the script you're about to write will execute when the playback head reaches Frame 30.

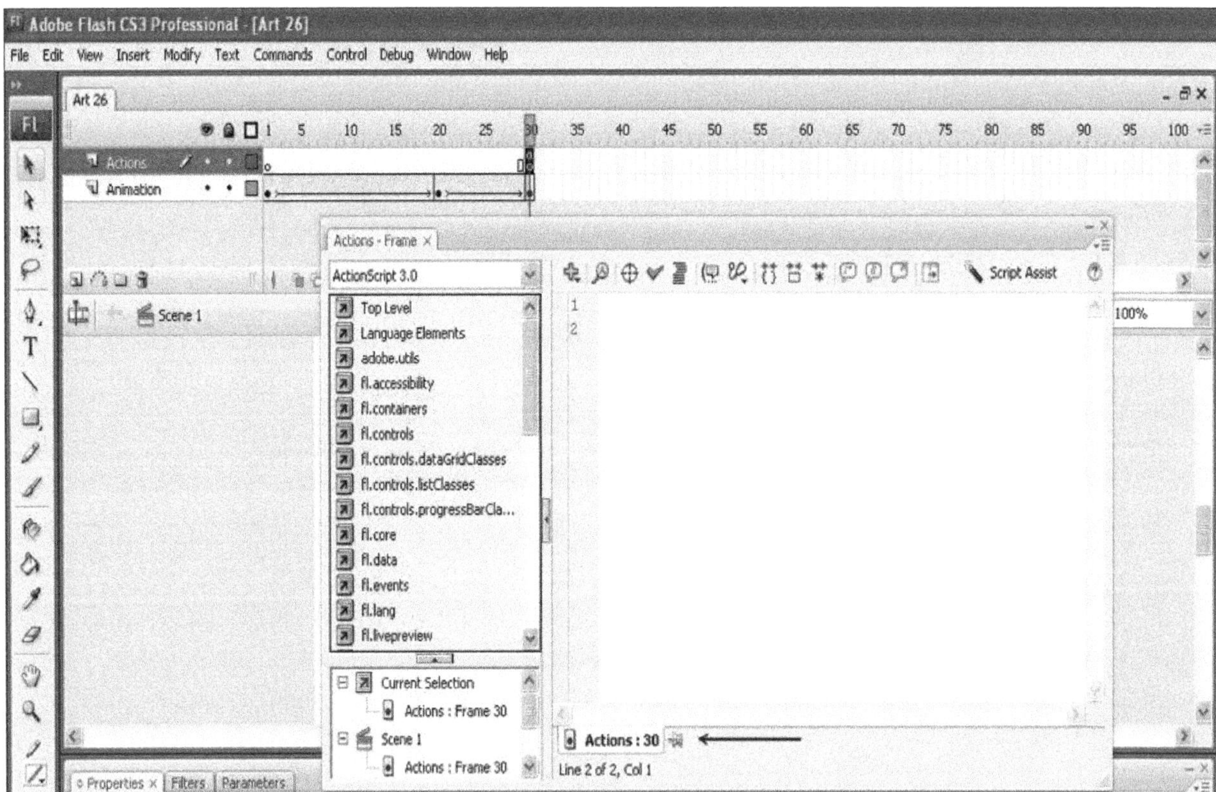

Picture 7.3

6. From Script Category dropdown, select ActionScript 1.0 & 2.0, select Global Functions from Toolbox, then select Timeline Control, and then double-click **gotoAndPlay**. You should see gotoAndPlay action added to your script in the Script pane on the right side. See picture 7.4. Because this action requires parameters, a code hint will appear to help guide you. In case it goes away, just click inside the parentheses following gotoAndPlay and click the Show Code Hint button.

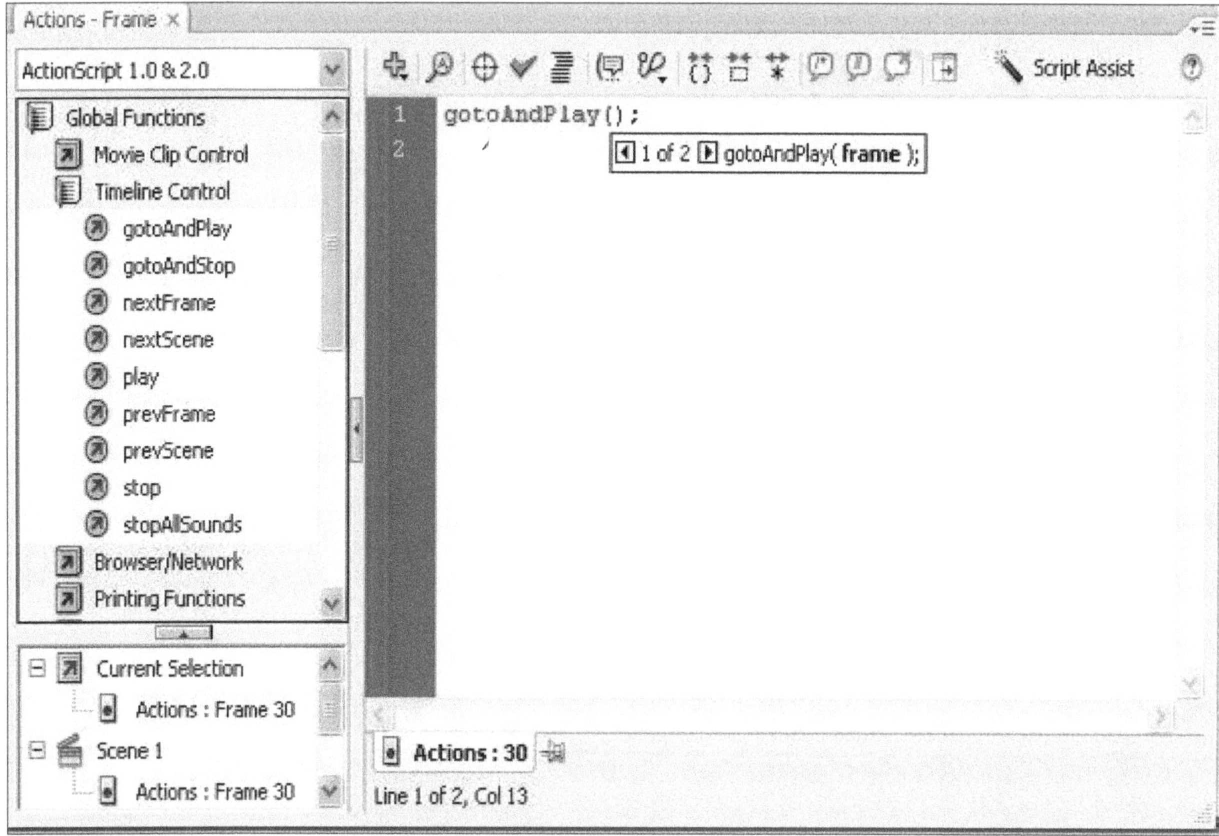

Picture 7.4

7. Now inside the parentheses type **20** because that's the frame numer to which you want to go and play. Therefore, the finished action in the script area should read
gotoAndPlay (20);

8. Close ActionScript box, save the file and test the movie by pressing Ctrl + Enter. Save this file for next lesson.

Lesson 27
Use a Frame Label for a gotoAndPlay **Action**

In this lesson you'll improve the gotoAndPlay action by supplying a frame label instead of a frame number.

1. Open the same .fla file you created in preceding lesson and click Frame 20 of the Animation layer. You're going to label this frame. In Properties panel, the box which is down below the Frame option, type **Loop Start**. See picture 7.5 and the arrow in it for help.

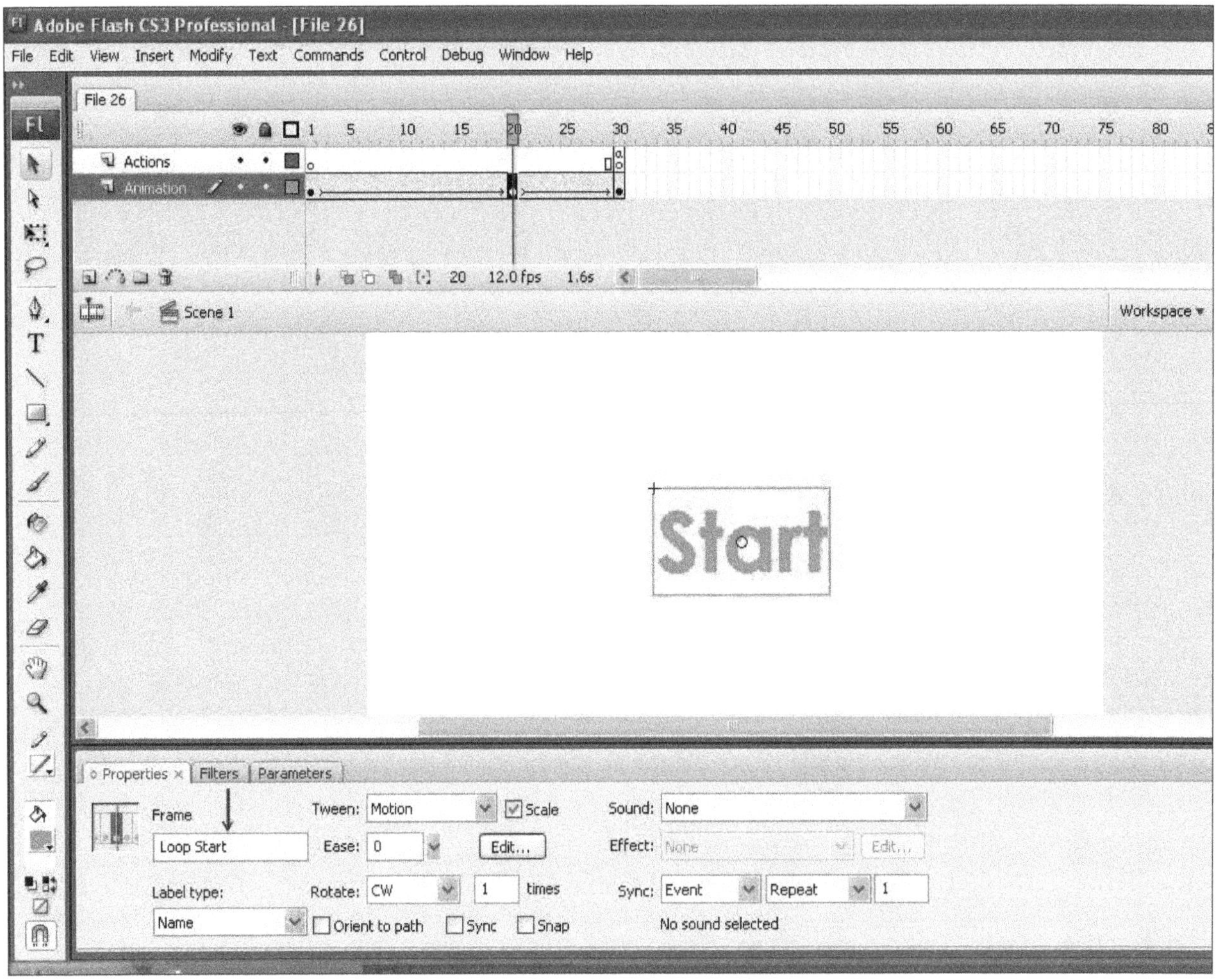

Picture 7.5

2. Click Frame 30 in the Actions layer and open the Actions panel. You're going to modify the gotoAndPlay line in the Actions panel. Change 20 to **"Loop Start"** (with the quotation marks). As shown in picture 7.6, the final script should read:

gotoAndPlay("Loop Start");

Picture 7.6

3. If you test the movie, it won't look different from the old version. Now go back to Animation layer, click Frame 20, and click and drag it so Loop Start is now at Frame 10, as shown in picture 7.7.

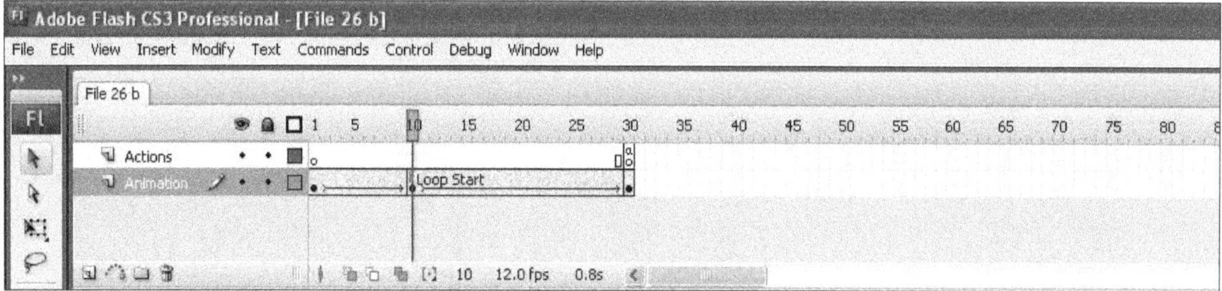

Picture 7.7

4. Press enter (not Ctrl + Enter) to play the animation on Flash's stage and you'll see that now the animation loops back to Frame 10, where you moved the Loop Start keyframe. The power of using a label is to moving it to any location you want. Save this file for next lesson.

Lesson 28
Display Current Time in Your Animation

The following lesson is pretty easy, as using ActionScript you can add a real-time clock in your animation.

1. Open Flash program as usual selecting (ActionScript 3.0), and save this new (blank) file in .fla extension.

2. Pick up the Text tool and set Text Type to Dynamic Text using Properties panel. Create a block of text setting the margin wide enough to accommodate at least 10 characters for the time. In the text block what you'll type will be replaced with the actual time. Go ahead and type something like: 12 : 01 : 35

3. Select the text block using Selection tool and use the Properties to give the text an Instance Name: clock_txt. See picture 7.8 for help.

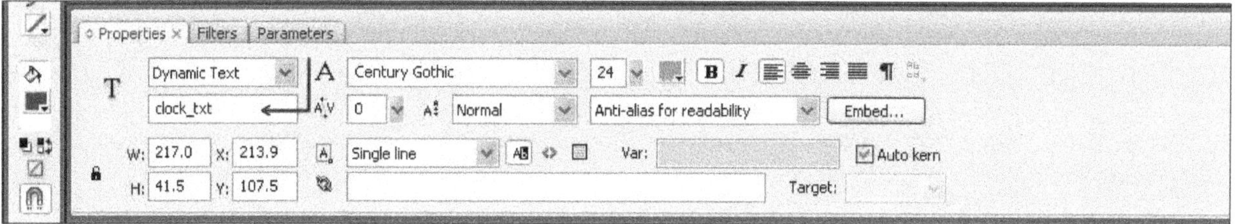

Picture 7.8

4. Click any cell in the Timeline and then open Actions panel. Type the following code into the panel:

```
addEventListener("enterFrame", updateClock);
function updateClock( evt ){
        var now = new Date ();
        clock_txt.text = now.toTimeString();
}
```

6. Test the movie pressing Ctrl + Enter and you'll see the time appear in you dynamic text field updating every second.

Lesson 29
Add Start and Stop Buttons to Your Animation

In this lesson you'll add buttons that can stop and continue the animation on screen. Please follow these steps for that:

1. Open the same .fla Flash file or create one with a motion tween over several frames.

2. Insert a new layer for buttons and name the layer Buttons.

3. Into the Button layer at Frame 1, draw a red-color rectangle that will become stop button. Draw another green-color rectangle that will become start button. Select the red button, covert to symbol, name it MyButton1, and make sure the behavior is set to <u>Button</u>. Select the green button, covert to symbol, name it MyButton2, and make sure the behavior is set to <u>Button</u>.

4. Select red button again, go to Properties, and give it an instance name **stopButton**, then select green button and give it an instance name **startButton**. Make sure you type it properly as instructed.

5. Now you'll write the code for stop button. Select the same Frame 1 of Button layer and open Actions panel. Write the following code:

```
stopButton.addEventListener ( MouseEvent.CLICK, myStopHandler )
function myStopHandler( evt ) {
        stop ()
}
```

6. If you test the movie (Ctrl + Enter) now, by pressing red button you can stop the animation. I believe you'll like it. Close the test movie .swf file and go back to the first frame of the Button layer. Now you should write the code for start button. Open Actions panel and type the following:

```
startButton.addEventListener ( MouseEvent.CLICK, myStartHandler )
function myStartHandler( evt ) {
        play ()
}
```

7. Test the movie now. I'm sure both of the buttons would respond in order to start and playback the animation.

There is thousands of coding for ActionScipt in Flash, and this book is too small to cover all of them. I just showed you the way how it works. In the next lesson, I will include a few more coding which are easy and simple. I hope everything is still OK with you, because now you'd have understood that though ActionScript is hard but it widely used in animation.

Lesson 30
Import and Use Video in Flash

This is going to be very interesting lesson for you. In Flash, you can import, trim, edit and compress videos that keep the small and quality high. You can save the edited video as .flv file and play in Flash Player, and you'll see how you can publish the same video to Web also. There's a great work ahead!

1. To increase the types of video your computer will support, install QuickTime (from www.quicktime.com), and DirectX 9 or later (from www.microsoft.com/directx/). The reason why you install this two software is that Flash compresses and decompresses the videos at the time of importing and giving output. It needs Codec for that processing. Flash supports QuickTime (.mov), Digital Video (.dv), MPEG (.mpg or .mpeg), Windows Media (.asf or .wmv), and Videos for Windows (.avi) video formats.

2. Here for this lesson I'm going to use a four-minute long .avi format video clip. Go to File> Import> Import Video and select your Original Video Clip (it shouldn't be too long, don't put three-hour long entire movie in it or else you'll have to sit all day while it imports). Click next and in Deployment dialog box select the option that says Embed Video in SWF and play in timeline, and click next.

3. In Embedding dialog box, leave all the option as it is except last one. Select the last option – Edit the video first, and go to next. You'll have the part of your screen looking like picture 7.9.

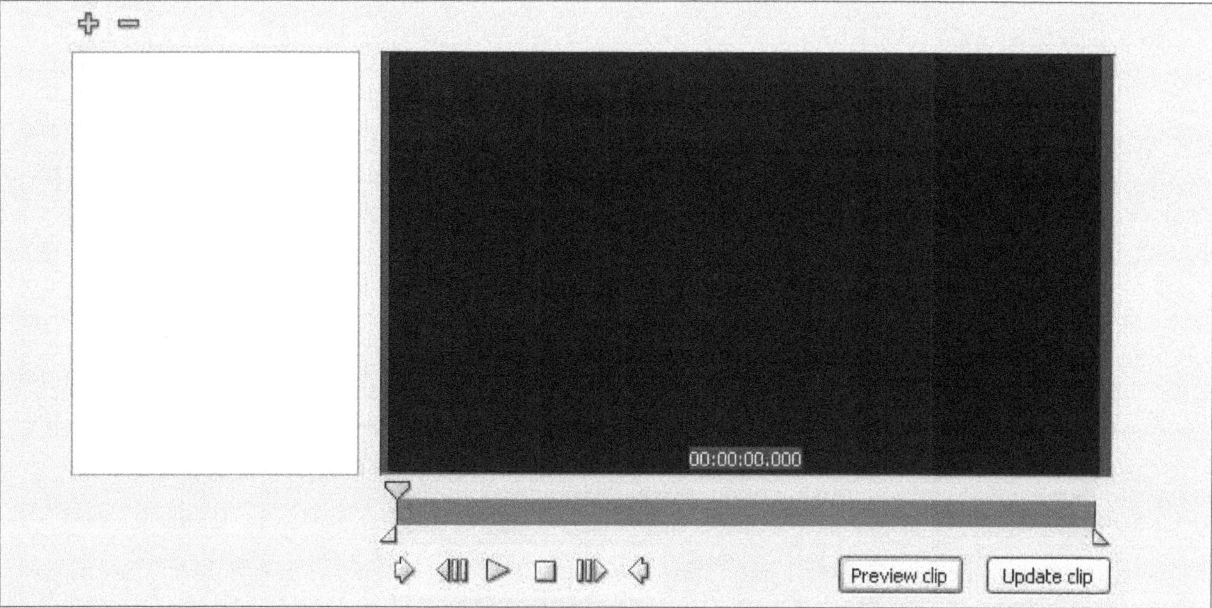

Picture 7.9

4. Movie trimming (cutting) is very easy here. Drag left and right trimmer button or hold Ctrl key down and drag the left of right corner of the clip line to cut. When done, place + or – button to set the trimmer button fixed. Only then you'll have Next button highlighted. Click Next.

5. Click next again on Encoding page and then select Finish. Now sit for a while and let it get encoded so that it could be ready for editing, formatting, and going to Web. The video will automatically come on the Stage and show on the Timeline.

6. Now let's add some standard video buttons that give the viewer a way to control the video. You're about to create the buttons (Stop, Pause, and Play). Lock this video layer and insert a new layer for buttons. Instead of drawing your own buttons select Windows> Common Libraries> Buttons. Inside the Library is a folder called Playback Rounded. Double click on it and drag each of the following buttons from that folder to the Stage: Rounded Green Pause, Rounded Green Play, and Rounded Green Stop. You can align them the way you want.

7. Use Properties to give your buttons the following instance names: pauseButton, playButton, and stopButton. Select Frame 1 of button layer and open Actions panel. Enter the following code in the Actions panel:

```
stop()
pauseButton.addEventListener("click", doPause)
playButton.addEventListener("click", doPlay)
stopButton.addEventListener("click", doStop)

function doPause ( evt ) {
        stop()
}
function doPlay ( evt ) {
        play()
}
function doStop ( evt ) {
        gotoAndStop(1)
}
```

8. If you haven't done any mistake in entering the code, then go ahead and test the movie and you'll see that all the three buttons are working. Save this as .fla file naming Edit Part One so that you can use it later.

9. In the process of editing video in Flash, you may need to save your edited output as .flv format so that you can play in Flash Player. For that, close and restart Flash. Go to File> Import> Import Video and select your Original Video Clip. Click next, on Deployment page select first option – Progressive download from a web server. You have to click next three times and then click finish. It'll ask to enter a name so type – Edit Part Two and save it on desktop (or wherever you like). After encoding process ends, you'll find your video in .flv format on desktop.

10. Now the last part of this lesson is publishing the video on Web. Close Flash entirely and start again. Open the Edit Part One .fla video file that you made in step 8 a little while ago (don't open Edit Part Two .flv file).

11. Go to File> Publish Settings. Make sure that on Publish Settings dialog box first two options Flash (.swf) and HTML (.html) are checked. Leave other options unchecked and click Publish. It'll take time. When done, click OK.

12. For your surprise, now you have total five files on desktop. If you double click the .html file, your video will start playing in your internet browser (Internet Explorer). To publish this video on Web (that you'll later in detail), you'll need all four files - .flv, .swf, .html and AC_RunActiveContent. You won't need .fla for Web.

Going Extra Mile
You can draw anything on your video. You want to know how? Fine, open the same Edit Part One .fla video. Create a new layer above video layer and name it Draw. Click on the word Draw to select the entire span of frames and press F6. Now you'll have Draw layer filled with empty keyframes where you can draw. Select Frame 1 of Draw layer, draw anything you want (frame, face, line), press (>) key which

is the <u>period key</u> to go to next frame and draw the same or do Paste in Place. Like this you can draw on all frames. That's it! Test the movie again.

Things to Remember
In addition to using Flash to compress videos in the .flv format, you can use outside Flash Video Editor to create .flv directly. That is Adobe Flash Video Encoder already installed in your computer. Developing your Flash video editing skills can help you become a professional movie editor and then you will use the programs like Adobe After Effects, Apple FinalCut Pro, Avid Xpress DV, Maya, and Combustion. Remember that two biggest factors that have an immediate impact on the file size are the video's framerate and its pixel dimensions. For example, a 12 fps video will be nearly exactly half the size as a 24 fps video. But a lower framerate video will not look as good as higher framerate's when there is a lot of motion. You can change the framerate from Properties and see what happens.

Lesson 31
Linking a Movie to the Web

The publish feature of Flash is both simple and quick. You can preview your video also by going to File> Publish Preview> Default (or press F12). Basically, you just select File> Publish and it not only exports a .swf, but it also creates the HTML and JavaScript files that are necessary. An HTML file is a text file that uses special code to describe how a web page is to be displayed. A viewer's browser first downloads the HTML code. JavaScript is a programming language that an HTML file can trigger to perform special behaviors on the browser such as resizing a window's size or changing its position. Playing Flash inside Internet Explorer requires some JavaScript code to overcome the default behavior of a video. Flash automatically creates the HTML file for you, so you don't really have to learn HTML. Remember that if you simply save or upload the .html, .js, and .swf files to a computer or web server, anyone can see your movie, provided the viewer has Flash player in their computer. You can make your own computer also a web server after your Internet Service Provider gives you the permission and you buy the space on Web from Satellite Service Provider. If you're done with this, your video will be live to the world on your own website.

At present people are more inclined to upload their videos on Youtube and give a URL of that on their websites. Though it serves the purpose but you lose the credibility of your site. I have seen that some people create their websites using still features already enabled by some web hosting companies. I agree to the point that this way one can put a company's identity on Web but ultimately the screen looks like a webpage, not a website. Because a website involves a lot of features including self owned audio, video, pages, sheets and current update. And that is why all these things are done by a web designer who is skilled in web programming like HTML, CSS, JavaScript, and it may need an animator skilled in Flash, Image Designing Software, Dreamweaver, and 3ds Max.

Creating a Hyperlink
A hyperlink is just a word or static picture in a web page that you can click to navigate to another web page. In Flash you can put hyperlinks on buttons or even in keyframes. This way, the viewer will have a chance to jump to other parts of the Web.

In this lesson you'll create a button that, when clicked, takes the viewer to another website. Here are the steps to follow:

1. First you can create a folder on desktop and name it Web Folder so that it can keep all the files you'll export from Flash. It will save files from getting scattered.

2. Open a new file clicking on AS 3.0. Go to Windows> Component and click on the + sign of User Interface. Drag a Button component onto the Stage as shown in picture 8.0. Go to Parameters tab in Properties and change this button's Label parameter to Go (that means type **Go** next to Label).

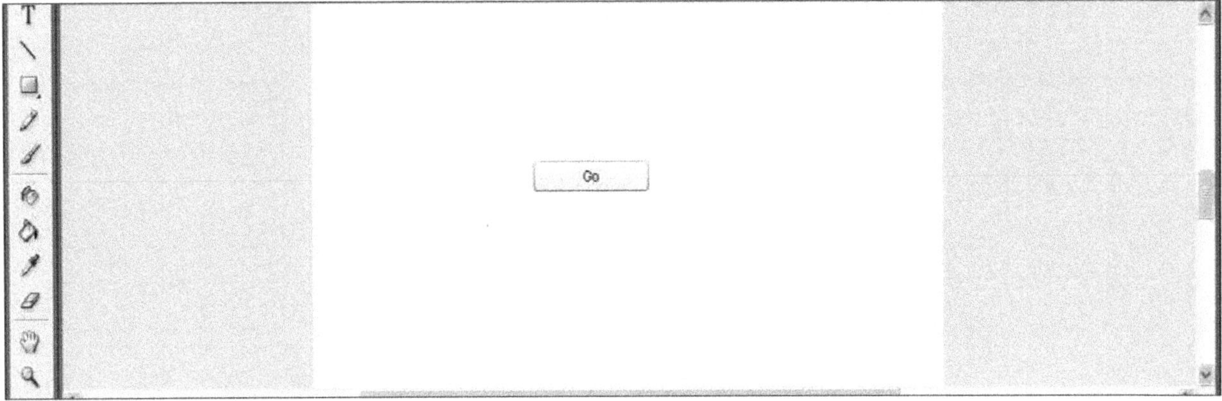

Picture 8.0

3. Click on Properties tab and give the Button component the instance name **goButton**. Click the keyframe, open the Actions panel and type the following code:

```
goButton.addEventListener(MouseEvent.CLICK, goNow)
function goNow ( evt ) {
        var url = "http://wwww.facebook.com/cromosys"
        navigateToURL( new URLRequest(url) )
}
```

4. Test the movie now. Click on the Go button, it will open the website.

Create a Text Hyperlink
You have already leant in this lesson how to create a button hyperlink. Now if you want to create a text hyperlink, then create a block of text using any font. Just make sure the block is big enough to accommodate a URL. With the text block selected, set text type to Static from Properties. In the URL Link field (next to the chain-link icon), type a correct URL. See picture 8.1 for help. When you test the movie and click on this text hyperlink, it'll open the website.

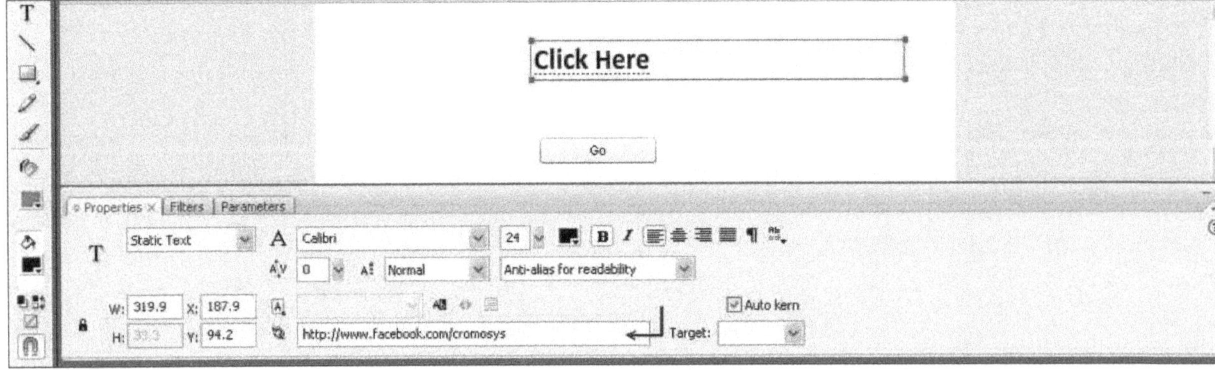

Picture 8.1

Lesson 32
Using Style Sheets

The teaching of Flash includes some parts of Web Designing also. For Web Designing, one needs to learn XHTLM, JavaScript, and CSS (Cascading Style Sheets). You can use CSS to define text style like a word processor. When you change the CSS definition, the text that uses the style automatically updates. Its definition can be stored within Flash or in external .css files.

Displaying Text by Using CSS
In this lesson you'll control text display by using CSS code which you'll type in Notepad. Follow the instructions and type the code carefully as even a single mistake will not let you go ahead.

1. Make a new folder on desktop and name it CSS. Open Notepad and type this code accurately:

```
bodyText {
    font-family: Verdana;
    color:#000000;
    font-size: 10px;

}
headline {
    font-family: Verdana;
    color:#006600;
    font-size: 24px;

}
a:hover{
    color:#FF0000;
    font-size: 10px;
    text-decoration:underline;

}
```

2. Save this text file in CSS folder naming it styles.css. When you save it, you'll the icon comes up with a wheel symbol. And if you place you mouse pointer on styles.css icon, it will say Cascading Style Sheet Document. I have directly copied and pasted this code from my program file, so there is no chance of typing mistake from my end. Please you make sure you've typed the code correct.

3. Create a new Flash AS 3.0 Flash file and save it in the same CSS folder naming it usesCSS.fla. It is must. Don't save it anywhere else or give any other name. When these two files are in same folder only then they can interact to each other.

4. Place onstage a dynamic text filed and make the margins as wide as the stage. Select and give this text filed an instance name myCssText_txt. There is no need to type any letter in the field.

5. Select the first keyframe, open the Actions panel, and type the following code:

```
//clear the text field:
myCssText_txt.text = ""
//define a new style sheet and attach it to the text field
var myStyles:StyleSheet = new StyleSheet()
myCssText_txt.styleSheet = myStyles
//set up the URL loader to read the css file
var myURLLoader:URLLoader = new URLLoader()
myURLLoader.addEventListener(Event.COMPLETE, stylesLoaded)
//define what happens when it loads
function stylesLoaded (evt) {
//parse the css file
myStyles.parseCSS( myURLLoader.data )
//populate the field using our new styles
myCssText_txt.htmlText = "<headline>this is the headline</headline>"
myCssText_txt.htmlText += "<bodyText>this is the body</bodyText>"
myCssText_txt.htmlText += "<bodyText>this is a "
myCssText_txt.htmlText += "<a href='#'>link</bodyText>"

}
//commence loading
myURLLoader.load (new URLRequest( "styles.css") )
```

6. Test the movie now. It will open like a page with the word "link" in the last line hyperlinked, which if clicked, will open a website.

When you want your creation to put on a web server, you should know how it works. A web server is a computer that is connected to the Internet and is configured to let other view files through common Internet browser. It needs a right kind of connection with server software installed. The process of uploading is simple – you just copy the .swf and .html files in the same location to the hard drive of the server. In the process of that you'll need a File Transfer Protocol (FTP) program. The software program Dreamweaver has a built-in feature to upload files.

Lesson 33
Designing a Website to Be Modular

It is possible to create a huge website entirely with one giant Flash file. However, separating the site into modular segments has distinct advantages. You can put several videos with their images in the modular.

1. Create a folder on desktop and name it Modular. Open Flash AS 3.0 and create a small animation apply motion effect you like. Save this file in Modular folder naming it Red.fla. Export this video and save it in the same folder naming it Red.swf. Close and restart Flash, create another (different) animation, and then save it in the same folder naming it Green.fla and export and save its .swf file naming it Green.swf. Close and restart Flash, create one more (different) animation, and then save it in the same folder naming it White.fla and export and save its .swf file naming it White.swf. Now you have total six files in Modular folder.

2. Close Flash entirely and start again and save this file also in the same folder naming it main.fla. Draw a no-fill square exactly 300x300 using the Info panel to change its dimension to 300x300. Make sure it is a rectangle line only and there is no color filled in it. Select the entire outline and covert to it a symbol. Make it a Movie Clip, name it box, and select the top-left Registration option in the same Behavior dialog box. With the box selected, name the instance **myClip**.

3. Drag a Button component onto the stage and give it an instance name **redButton**. Use the Parameters tab to change the button's label to **Red**. Select Frame 1 in timeline, open the Actions panel, and type the following code.

```
var myLoader:Loader = new Loader()
myClip.addChild( myLoader )
redButton.addEventListener(MouseEvent.CLICK , clickRed)
function clickRed ( evt ){
        myLoader.load( new URLRequest("red.swf") )
}
```

4. Drag two more buttons, put the instance name **greenButton** and **whiteButton** and change their labels to **Green** and **White**. Add the remaining part of code as it is easy to type because the second and third section of code is similar of the first.

```
greenButton.addEventListener(MouseEvent.CLICK , clickGreen)
function clickGreen ( evt ){
        myLoader.load( new URLRequest("green.swf") )
}
whiteButton.addEventListener(MouseEvent.CLICK , clickWhite)
function clickWhite ( evt ){
        myLoader.load( new URLRequest("white.swf") )
}
```

4. Test the movie now; I am sure it'll work. This way, in addition to loading .swf files, you can load .jpg, gif and .png images also.

Lesson 34
Playing External Sounds

You can play MP3 sounds that reside outside a movie. This lesson shows how to make a jukebox application.

1. Find a few MP3 files and place them in a new folder. Name the files song1.mp3, song2.mp3, and song3.mp3.

2. Create a new Flash file and save it as jukebox.fla in the same folder where the MP3s reside. Drag a List component onto the Stage and give it an instance name **songList**.

3. Select Frame 1 in timeline, open Actions panel and enter this code:

```
songList.addItem( {label: "Title of song one", filename: "song1.mp3" } )
songList.addItem( {label: "Title of song two", filename: "song2.mp3" } )
songList.addItem( {label: "Title of song three", filename: "song3.mp3" } )

songList.addEventListener(Event.CHANGE, playSong)
var mySound:Sound
var soundChannel:SoundChannel;
function playSong( evt ){
        if (soundChannel != null ){
                soundChannel.stop()
                }
                mySound = new Sound()
                mySound.load( new URLRequest ( songList.selectedItem.filename ) )
                soundChannel = mySound.play()
                }
```

4. That's it! If you have right kind of MP3 in the new folder, then definitely it would play when you test the movie.

Lesson 35
Advanced Animation Techniques

As a magician creates an illusion and the viewers believe the result, in the same way an animator also creates an illusion when he or she applies advanced techniques. Watching a series of still images can make you believe you're watching something move, but in reality nothing moves. In this lesson you're going to use the Drop Shadow filter to add a blurred trail to a simple object.

Add a Motion Blur
1. In a new file, draw a filled circle, select it, and covert it to a symbol naming **Circle** with Movie Clip behavior.

2. Move this instance of the Circle to the left side of the Stage. In Frame 25, insert a keyframe (F6). In Frame 30, insert a frame (F5).

3. In Frame 10, insert a keyframe (F6), hold shift and drag the install all the way to the right side of the Stage. Now go to Frame 15 and insert another keyframe (F6).

4. Select the keyframe 1 and set Motion Tween, select keyframe 15 and there also set Motion Tween. Test the movie with no blur effect. Now we will start blur effect editing interpolated keyframes.

5. Click the cell in Frame 5 and insert a new keyframe (F6) and then again in Frame 20. Click in Frame 5 and select the instance onstage. Go to Filters and add a Blur filter. Double click the padlock to unlock the Blur X and Blur Y and set Blur X to 20 and Blur Y to 5. Select the instance in Frame 20 and add a Blur filter with the same settings. Test the movie to see the change which is not final.

6. Now we'll add a Drop Shadow. For that, select the instance onstage in Frame 5 and add a Drop Shadow. Set Blur X to 70 and Blur Y to 10, and change the shadow color to a little lighter.

Finally, set the angle to 180 and distance to 30. Select the instance in Frame 20 and apply the same Drop Shadow settings except set the **angle to 0** this time.

7. Just one more step is left. Select the instance onstage in Frame 1, access the Drop Shadow and set the angle to 180 – and do the same for Frame 10. Select the instance onstage in Frame 15, go to Drop Shadow and set the angle to 0 and repeat for Frame 25. Test the movie now and I'm sure you'll like it. You may apply Ease Out effect on Frame 5 and 20, if you wish.

Lesson 36
Using Anticipation

To draw the attention of the viewer to something that's about to happen, you can use anticipation. For example, a car with a manual transmission that is stopped facing up a hill drifts back a little bit when it begins to move forward. You can accentuate that effect in your animations to make them more effective. Not only will the viewers look at the objects that's preparing to move (by moving in the opposite direction), but they'll anticipate that something's about to happen.

1. In a new file, draw a filled circle at the bottom of the Stage and convert it to a symbol naming Circle with behavior set to Movie Clip.

2. Insert a keyframe at Frame 10, then other at 15, and one more at 25. You will squash the circle in the next step between Frames 10 and 15 and then move it up as it goes to Frame 25.

3. First select Frame 25, hold down Shift key and then move the instance of Circle close to the top of the Stage.

4. In Frame 10, use the Free Transform tool to compress the circle by scaling it vertically. Also make it a little wider because when you squash something in real life, it gets wider too. If you hold down Alt key while you drag the top-middle resizing handle, the bottom of the circle won't move. You can keep Onion Skin on while doing that.

5. In Frame 15, do the same with the Circle but all in the opposite direction. Select keyframe 10 and set Motion Tween. Then select keyframe 15 and apply the same Motion effect.

6. You can test the movie now, but to make it more believable, make Circle snap into its normal shape as soon as it starts to move. For that, go to Frame 16 and insert a keyframe, select the Circle and go to Modify> Transform> Remove Transform. The Circle immediately returns to its un-scaled state. Test the movie now and keep the .fla file saved. Now you've understood that if you're moving something to the right, adding a slight move to the left draw the attention of the viewers.

Using Overkill
Anticipation happens before the animation plays, and overkill applies to the end of an animation. If you're in a car that comes to a stop, you fee as though you move backward just for a moment after the car comes to a rest. This kind of effect is called Overkill that makes the animation more believable.

Open the same .fla file of this lesson that you saved before. Insert keyframes in Frames 26, 27, and 28 by clicking in Frame 26 and then pressing F6 three times. In Frame 26, stretch the Circle taller by half an inch. In Frame 27, move the Circle down from its Frame 25's position. Test the movie now and see what Overkill does.

Animation truly is a matter of fooling the viewer! To prove this, imagine an animation with no tweening but with anticipation and overkill. Draw a circle at the bottom in Frame 1, enable (F6) keyframe 10 and squash the circle. In Frame 20, move the circle half way up the Stage. In Frame 12 stretch it a little, in Frame 27 squash it again, and in Frame 28 put it back in its normal shape. Test the movie, and it'll look great without tweening.

Lesson 37
Simulating Depth and Perspective

1. You're going to draw same moving car. Despite the fact that Flash is only a two-dimensional program, you can still make the user think your movies have the depth. In this lesson you'll add just two lines to make the perspective more apparent. Draw a car following the same steps of lesson 19. Convert the entire instance of car to a Movie Clip symbol. In Frame 1, place the car in the bottom left of the Stage, add a keyframe in Frame 40, and move the car to the top right of the Stage. Do a simple Motion Tween between the keyframes.

2. Scale the car larger in Frame 1 and smaller in Frame 40. Insert a new layer and draw two converging lines as if they were the shoulders of a road as shown in picture 8.2.

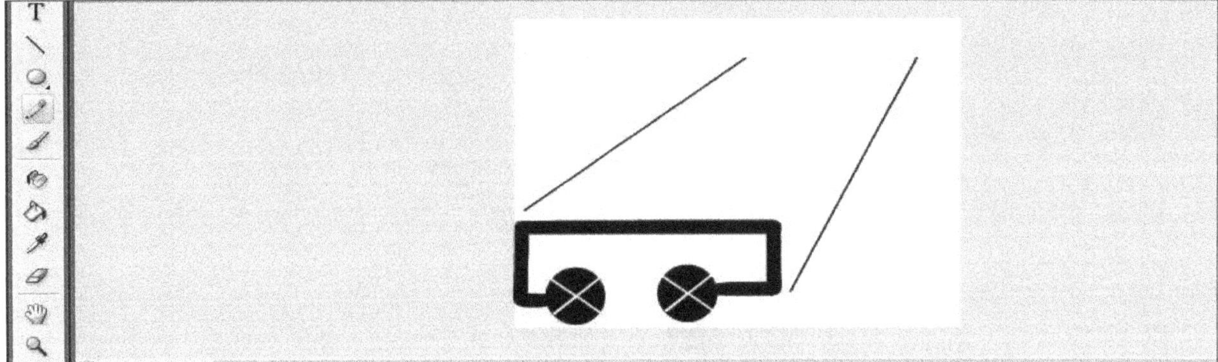

Picture 8.2

3. To add even more evidence that the car is covering great distances, add mountains in the road layers as shown in picture 8.3.

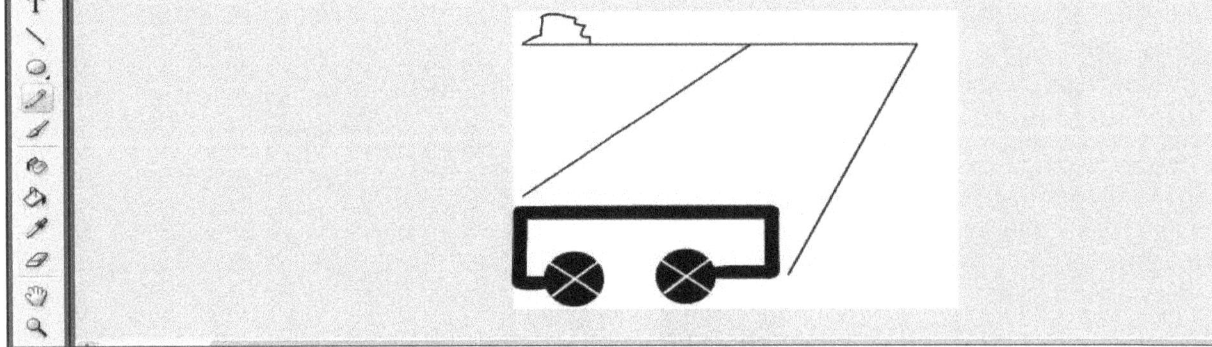

Picture 8.3

4. Here you can use your artistic skills and test the movie at the end. I am sure this animation will look move convincing. Like this, you can create many animations applying your creativity.

Though this book ends here but the world of Flash for you doesn't end here. You can still imagine and create new animations. Writing this book was one of the toughest jobs of my life especially putting images and ActionScript in this book. I believe I didn't leave any single stone unturned. If you make a move from here for learning Autodesk 3ds Max and Maya, you'll find my book soon available on Internet for that also.

Niranjan Jha Showman
Trainer, Author, Physician, Entrepreneur, Filmmaker, Activist
Cromosys Corporation
Education and Technology Research Center
www.facebook.com/cromosys
+91-9561450045
Nallasopara (W), Mumbai, India

NIRANJAN JHA SHOWMAN

Founder - Niranjan Jha Showman

Education and Technology Research Center

Patankar Park, Nallasopara (W), Mumbai. +91-9561450045

Education, Technology, Publication, Healthcare, Newsmedia, Realtor, Filmmaking

www.facebook.com/cromosys

Cromosys Publication
Teach
Yourself
German
NIRANJAN JHA SHOWMAN

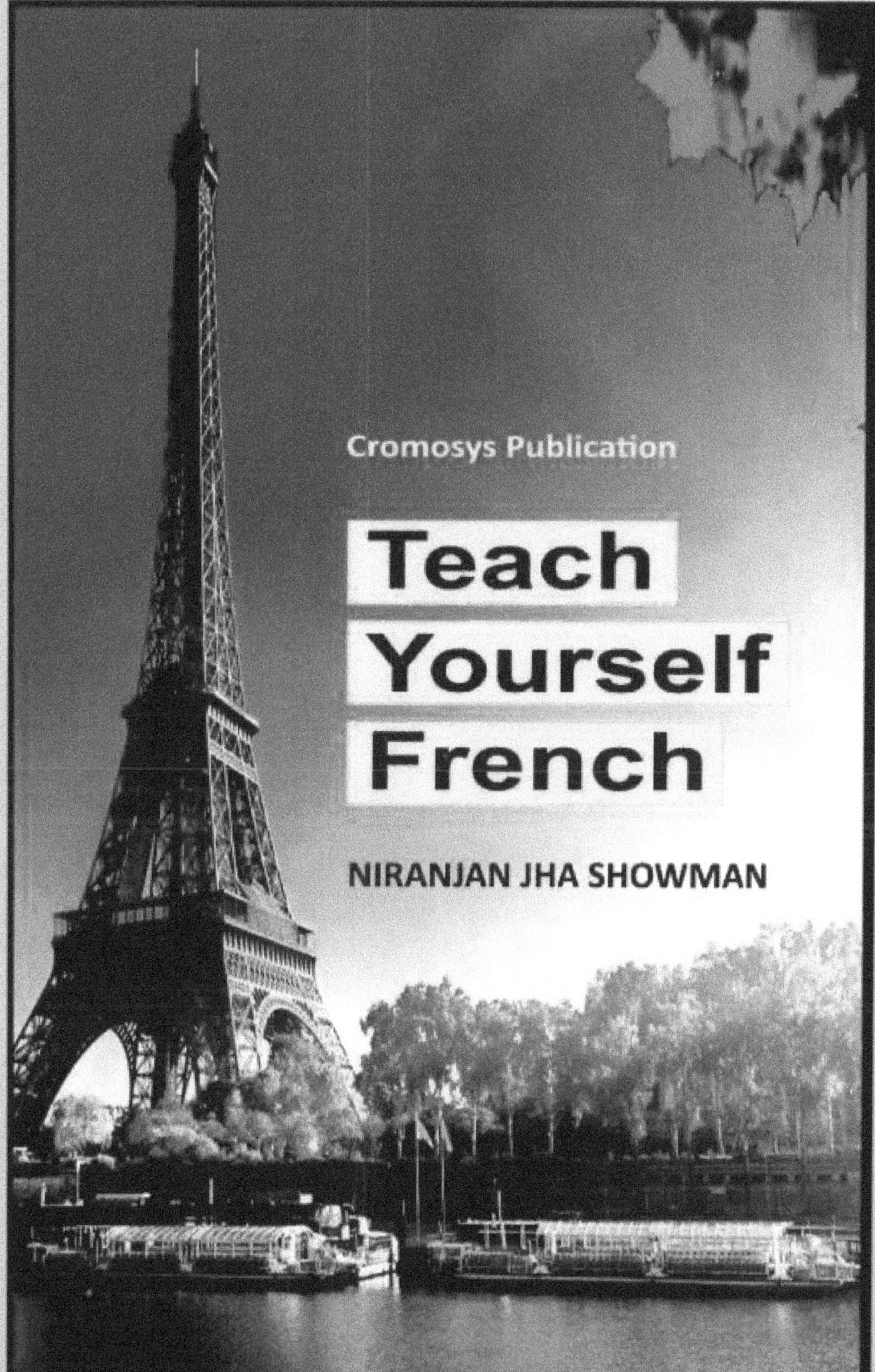

Cromosys Publication
Teach
Yourself
French
NIRANJAN JHA SHOWMAN

Cromosys Publication
Teach
Yourself
Spanish
NIRANJAN JHA SHOWMAN

Cromosys Publication

English
Voice
Accent and
Pronunciation

NIRANJAN JHA SHOWMAN

Teach
Yourself
Autodesk
MAYA
Cromosys Publication
NIRANJAN JHA SHOWMAN

Cromosys Publication
Teach
Yourself
Autodesk
3ds Max
NIRANJAN JHA SHOWMAN

Cromosys Publication
CRIMINAL FACTORY
NIRANJAN JHA SHOWMAN

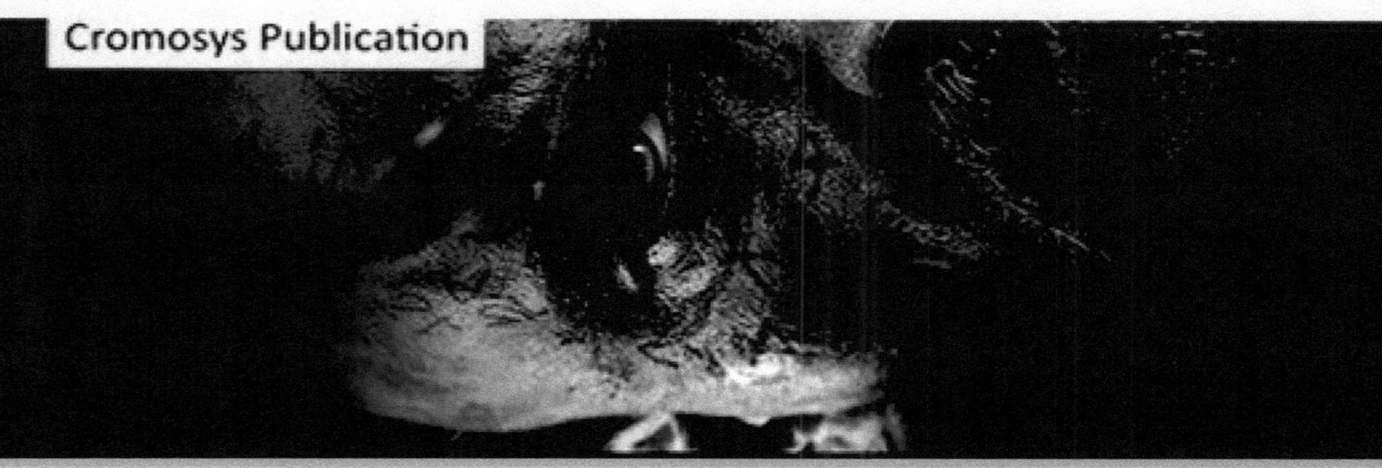

Cromosys Publication
NIRANJAN JHA SHOWMAN
FOCAL DISASTER

Cromosys Publication
Your talents will not help you succeed without your skill of using them.
NIRANJAN JHA SHOWMAN
BE
MILLIONAIRE
LIKE
ME

Extracts from the Register of Copyrights

Dated : 16/08/2022

1.	Registration Number	:	**T-87782-2022**
2.	Name, address and nationality of the applicant	:	NIRANJAN JHA SHOWMAN, CROMOSYS PUBLICATION, 001, JAYSATYAM, PATANKAR ROAD, NALLASOPARA (W), MUMBAI, MAHARASHTRA - 401203. INDIAN
3.	Nature of the applicant's interest in the copyright of the work	:	AUTHOR
4.	Class and description of the work	:	LITERARY / BOOK
5.	Title of the work	:	**Teach Yourself Adobe Flash**
6.	Language of the work	:	ENGLISH
7.	Name, address and nationality of the author and if the author is deceased, date of his decease	:	NIRANJAN JHA SHOWMAN, CROMOSYS PUBLICATION, 001, JAYSATYAM, PATANKAR ROAD, NALLASOPARA (W), MUMBAI, MAHARASHTRA - 401203. INDIAN
8.	Whether the work is published or unpublished	:	UNPUBLISHED
9.	Year and country of first publication and name, address and nationality of the publisher	:	N.A.
10.	Years and countries of subsequent publications, if any, and names, addresses and nationalities of the publishers	:	N.A. SAME AS ABOVE
11.	Names, addresses and nationalities of the owners of various rights comprising the copyright in the work and the extent of rights held by each, together with particulars of assignments and licences, if any	:	
12.	Names, addresses and nationalities of other persons, if any, authorised to assign or licence of rights comprising the copyright	:	N.A.
13.	If the work is an 'Artistic work', the location of the original work, including name, address and nationality of the person in possession of the work. (In the case of an architectural work, the year of completion of the work should also be shown).	:	N.A.
14.	If the work is an 'Artistic work', whether it is registered under the Designs Act 2000 if yes give details.	:	N.A.
15.	If the work is an 'Artistic work', capable of being registered as a design under the Designs Act 2000.whether it has been applied to an article though an industrial process and ,if yes ,the number of times it is reproduced.	:	N.A.
16.	Remarks, if any	:	

Diary Number :   8523/2020-DF/T
Date of Application :   25/07/2020
Date of Receipt :   25/07/2020

DEPUTY REGISTRAR OF COPYRIGHTS